William John Loftie

Views in North Wales

From original drawings

William John Loftie

Views in North Wales
From original drawings

ISBN/EAN: 9783337329105

Printed in Europe, USA, Canada, Australia, Japan

Cover: Foto ©Andreas Hilbeck / pixelio.de

More available books at **www.hansebooks.com**

VIEWS IN NORTH WALES

FROM

ORIGINAL DRAWINGS BY T. L. ROWBOTHAM

MEMBER OF THE SOCIETY OF PAINTERS IN WATER-COLORS

WITH

Archæological, Historical, Poetical, and Descriptive Notes

COMPILED BY

THE REV. W. J. LOFTIE, B.A., F.S.A.

AUTHOR OF "A CENTURY OF BIBLES," "THE LATIN YEAR," ETC., ETC.

New York:

SCRIBNER, WELFORD, & ARMSTRONG, BROADWAY

LONDON: MARCUS WARD & CO.

1875

CONTENTS.

CHROMOGRAPHS.

INITIAL VIGNETTES.

S N O W D O N.

THE highest mountain in England and Wales, Snowdon yet falls far short of Ben Nevis and Ben Muich Dhui across the Scottish border. Indeed, there are as many as sixteen or seventeen Caledonian peaks which exceed it, some of them by as much as eight hundred feet. On the other hand, there is no mountain in Ireland which approaches Snowdon by more than a hundred feet—Carrantuohill, in Kerry, the highest in the sister island, being only three thousand four hundred and fourteen, while Snowdon is three thousand five hundred and seventy-one feet above the waters of the intervening channel. This advantage is, moreover, set off by the position of the minor hills which surround Snowdon. Several of them, although of great altitude, are at a sufficient distance not to interfere with him; and while it is often difficult to say, in Highland or in Irish scenery, which is really the tallest in a chain of hills, there can never be a moment's doubt in the presence of Snowdon as to his supremacy among his compeers.

Before proceeding to describe the ascents which may be made, and to quote from the chief authors who have mentioned Snowdon, it may be well to say something as to the geographical and geological features of the district. Fortunately, very competent guides are at hand. It is, in fact, not very easy to select from a number of writers on the subject. The Lower Silurian rocks, of which the range mainly consists, have received much attention from geologists ; and if the student goes carefully over the ground, he will also find plain evidence of volcanic action, and "will perceive various patches of igneous eruptive rocks standing out from amidst the great Lower Silurian formation. Beginning from the north, he will be able to trace the great rugged Snowdonian range from Penmaenmawr to Moel Hebog, above Tremadoc. Singular as it appears, this range 'is composed of rocks which are the equivalents of the strata occupying the comparatively low-lying hills of the Bala district east of Arenig.' In other words, the lavas and volcanic ashes of this great chain were erupted in the Caradoc or Bala epoch. To the west of the flanks of this range we have, then, emerging from under these altered Caradoc strata, and much traversed by porphyries, Llandeilo beds, overlying the Lingula flags, beneath which again lie the great mass of Cambrian grits and slates which supply the quarries of Penrhyn and Llanberis. To the south of Moel Hebog we have the same series repeated, with the difference that the Lingula flags at Tremadoc abut upon the great Merionethshire mass of Cambrian rock. Immediately on the east of Snowdon is a narrow anticlinal axis of slate and sandstone, full of Caradoc or Bala fossils, which separates what may be called the great porphyritic basin of the Snowdon range from the minor basin of Dolwyddelau, of precisely the same age." The "Cambrian "

formation is also very well defined. It occurs in two separate
districts—one in Merionethshire, the other in Caernarvonshire. The
latter "commences between Bangor and Carnedd Llewelyn, and
terminates at the sea near Clynnog. 'Between the Menai Straits
and the east flank of the Snowdon range we find huge buttresses
of very ancient grit, schist, slate, and sandstone, having the same
direction from south-south-west to north-north-east, in which,
though their sedimentary character is obvious, and though they
have not been so much altered as in Anglesea, but one obscure
fossil has been detected throughout a thickness of many thousand
feet.'—*Murchison.* These rocks are the equivalents of the
Longmynd or Bottom rocks of Shropshire, and their commercial
importance will be duly estimated as being the *locale* of the
Llanberis and Penrhyn quarries." Some account of the slate
quarries will be found in our notice of Moel Siabod. The author
of *Siluria* says :—" ' The strata which constitute the lower part of
Snowdon itself, and repose upon the older slates and Lingula flags,
consist of dark bluish-grey slaty schists, representing the inferior
part of the Llandeilo formation. They are traversed by masses of
eruptive rock, consisting of porphyry and greenstone, or compact
felspar or felstone. In the next overlying accumulations are many
Caradoc fossils, although the original beds alternate rapidly with
volcanic dejections of ashes and felspathic materials.' Professor
Ramsay considers that most of the intruding bosses of greenstone,
porphyry, and syenite, which traverse the rocks west of the
Snowdon chain and the great Merionethshire district of Cambrian
rocks, &c., date about the close of the Lingula flag period—*i.e.*,
in the epoch of the Llandeilo rocks. A period of comparative

repose succeeded, followed by those eruptions which produced the
porphyries of Snowdon. 'All these Snowdonian porphyries,' he
says, 'are true lava-beds, accompanied by volcanic ashes of the
same period.' "

Professor Ramsay has published in a separate form his chapters
on Swiss and Welsh *Glaciers*, originally contributed to a volume
by the members of the Alpine Club. In his preface he says :—
" It is now twenty years since Agassiz and Buckland announced
that the valleys of the Highlands and of Wales had once been
filled with glaciers. Few but geologists heard the announcement,
and, with rare exceptions, those who cared at all about it, met the
glacial theory of the drift in general, and that of extinct glaciers in
particular, with incredulity, and sometimes with derision. Rash
writers still held that the far-borne boulder drift, so widely spread
over the cold and temperate regions of Europe and America, had
been scattered abroad by mighty sea waves, set in motion by the
sudden upheaval of hypothetical northern continents ; and the
polish and striation of the rocks in the mountain valleys—the
veritable signs of vanished glaciers—were attributed by flippant
writers and talkers to cart-wheels, hobnailed boots, and the nether
integuments of Welshmen sliding down the hills ; as if the country
had been inhabited by a monstrous race of primitive Celts—all
clad in the famous armour of stone worn by Loupgarou and his
giants, when they fought with the heroic Pantagruel—their sole
occupation for illimitable ages having consisted in the performance
of Titanic *glissades* upon the rocks. Now, however, the tide has
changed, and for years the glacial theory (applied to a late Tertiary
epoch in Britain and elsewhere) has not only steadily gained ground

among geologists, but has even found its way into the writings of more popular authors."

Speaking more immediately of Snowdon, he proceeds :—

"This mountain, the highest and noblest in the district, is bounded on three sides by valleys, which in all respects are unsurpassed in geological interest and wild beauty by any in North Wales. On the north-east lie the bare crags of the narrow Pass of Llanberis, on the east the softer beauties of Nant Gwynant, and on the west the long drift-covered slopes of the broad depression that runs from Llyn Cwellyn* to Beddgelert. In the midst of these, the mountain rises in a tall peak 3571 feet above the sea, its base being formed mostly of old lava-beds of felspathic porphyry, and the topmost thousand feet chiefly of stratified felspathic tuffs and ashes. In these rocks six vast hollows have been scooped by time, forming the wild upland valleys of Cwm-glas-bach, † Cwm-glas, Llyn Llydaw, ‡ Cwm-y-llan,§ Cwm-y-clogwyn,|| and Llyn du'r Arddu,¶ in some of which the

---

* *Cwellyn*, properly *Cawellyn*—a basket, hamper, or creel. So called from the fishing-creels once used in the lake. † Little Grey Valley.

‡ *Llydaw* is the Welsh name of Armorica, but there seems to be no sense in this interpretation. *Lludw* means *ashes* or *cinders*, and it is remarkable that on parts of the slopes round the lake, there are consolidated Lower Silurian volcanic ashes, still so scoriaceous-looking, that even a person who is no geologist might readily recognise them as volcanic.

§ The Enclosed Valley. || The Craggy Valley.

¶ *Gardd*, or *Ardd*, when preceded by the article *yr* (the), means a garden, and this name has often been translated the "lake of the black garden." Such a name, however, seems to have no sense when taken in connexion with the locality. *Arddu* also means " the extreme of blackness ;" and lying, as the pool does, in a deep hollow at the base of a tall black cliff, the name literally signifies "the blackest black lake," or, as it might be freely translated into Scotch, " Pitmirk Loch."

signs of glacier ice are even more striking than in the Pass of
Llanberis itself."

Professor Ramsay goes over each of these valleys separately,
and notes their peculiarities. Many of his descriptions are very
graphic, and of interest apart from their geological meaning.
Everywhere he sees signs of glacial action, and unconsciously, while
telling of the marks he can detect, he draws most accurate and real
pictures of the scenery. His little book, which contains an admir-
able map, is indispensable to every geologist who visits Snowdon ;
so we will only select one more passage as an example of the
learned professor's power of word-painting. He is speaking of the
valley on the eastern slope of Snowdon :—

" Approaching Llyn Llydaw, the full grandeur of this wonderful
valley bursts on the beholder. A lake rather more than a mile in
length, and of a green colour, like some of the lakes of Switzerland,
obliquely crosses the valley. Around it rise the cliffs of Lliwedd,
Crib Goch, and Pen Wyddfa, seamed with veins of white quartz that
gleam like streaks of snow on the tall black rocks circling the vast
amphitheatre, the scarred sides and ragged outlines of which,
sharply defined against the sky, may well seem, till attempted,
hopelessly inaccessible to the unpractised climber. In every season
and phase of weather there is a charm in this valley to the lover
of the mountains—in quiet sunshine, when the rocks, and perhaps
a lazy ferry-boat, are reflected in the still water ; or while the
wanderer scales the crags amid the seething mists ; or when the
pitiless rain, or hail, or snow, comes driving down the valley ; but
best of all, in a threatening evening, when the gathered clouds,
like the roof of a vast cavern, hang heavily from side to side on the

edges of hills, and a streak of light, caught from the setting sun, shows redly behind the dim peak of Snowdon, grimly reflected in the sombre waters of the lake.

"The signs of a glacier are so evident in Cwm Llydaw that it is needless to describe all the details. At the outflow of the lake there are moraine-like mounds, formed of earthy matter, stones, and angular and subangular blocks, which even now partly dam up the lake, and when I first knew it, raised it to a still higher level, ere the channel of the brook was sacrilegiously deepened to lower the water, for the sake of saving a few pounds in the construction of an ugly causeway. Close to the outflow, the once beautiful little islets of rock, feathered with heath and grasses, are now united to the mainland, and a broad ugly black rim round the lake marks alike the extent of the drainage and the barbarism of the perpetrators of this unhappy outrage on the most beautiful scene in Wales."

So much, then, for the geological features of Snowdonia. We will now endeavour to enumerate the principal points of ascent, and to describe those which are best worth attempting. In old times such an undertaking as a climb to the top of the mountain was considered in the highest degree perilous. But modern travellers make the ascent almost daily, only fearing a fog which may obscure their view, and, if they are without a guide, endanger their descent. Snowdon is particularly liable to sudden fogs; and the tourist not already well acquainted with the tracks does a foolhardy thing in going up alone. Many people, too, like to meet the sun on the summit, and must for that purpose make their journey by night. In no case should this be done without the assistance and direction of a well-skilled companion.

There are four distinct paths of ascent. They are those from Llanberis, which is the easiest; from Capel Curig, which is the longest and most tedious; from Beddgelert, which, from its including the famous pass of the Clawdd Goch, is perhaps the most picturesque; and the ascent from Llyn Cwellyn, which is not often made, but which includes a visit to the Maen Bras, of which Mr. Ramsay has much to say. It was from a cliff on this last route that Mr. Starr, a Northamptonshire clergyman, was killed in a fog, in November, 1846. He was well accustomed to ascend by himself, and on this occasion the guide attempted in vain to dissuade him. His body was not found for four months, during the winter, though constant search was made. When at last it was discovered, it had been much mangled, probably by wild cats or other vermin, and the head was lying at some distance from the body.

With regard to the name of Snowdon, we learn from Mr. Cliffe that it is a generic term. It is not properly applied to a particular mountain, but to a continuous tract of mountains. The word is Saxon, and evidently intends a hill where snow lies. The native appellation is *Eryri*, or *Craig Eryri*. Mr. Llwyd asserts that this term signifies eagles' rocks. Mr. Pennant assures us that the eagle is seldom seen here, and that the name, and the more modern one, Snowdon, are in fact synonymous, the latter being borrowed of the former. *Creigiau'r Eira*, he says, means *Snowy Mountains*, so named from the frequency of snow upon them. Pennant gives them up to snow from November to May, but sometimes they are powdered a little earlier or later. "In July, just after sunrise, the thermometer has been observed at 34 deg.,

and in August at 48 deg. early in the afternoon." The point of
permanent snow is about 4350 feet ; a considerably higher elevation
than Snowdon. In 1850, snow fell here in June ; sometimes it
falls early in October. One of Sir W. W. Wynn's mottoes is *Eryr
Eryrod Eryri*—" Eagle of the Eagles of Snowdon."

One of the titles of the Prince of Wales was " Lord of
Snowdon," and this mountain was regarded by the Welsh with
superstitious reverence, it being fabled that those who slept on it
would " wake inspired."

The ascent from Llanberis may first be described. A recent
writer, quoted by Mr. Cliffe, thus narrates his experience :—

" The morning was rather misty, but we were led to believe that
before we reached the summit it would clear up. Our road was
somewhat rough after we reached the first ascent : the path was
strewed over with the *débris* of the rocks, but the ponies
accustomed to this sort of travelling were quite as safe-footed as
our own horses are on a good turnpike road. The distance which
we had now to ascend was computed to be five miles, and a height
of 3571 feet ; but of this fact we never obtained a glimpse until we
had nearly completed our journey. Keeping on the side of the
vale of Cwm Brwynog, we threaded our path with comparative ease,
now and then scrambling over peaks of rocks which interspersed
our road, until we came upon Rushy Hollow. We now put our
animals upon a smart trot, passing over many a bog which in
winter would have swallowed us up. Here we met with a farmer,
who rented thousands of acres within our view, and a man of
substance, his wealth being estimated at least at £1500 capital,
having a flock of 200 sheep—a great number in that locality. His

dress certainly was a contrast to that of the English yeomen. Imagine a thin spare figure, with an old ' all round my hat,' with the brim off—which had once been white—with an old pair of corduroy breeches, without the knee-ties or buttons—a pair of brown woollen stockings, which once were black—and a light-coloured spare coat, with the nap worn by age, and ornamented here and there by a button or two of different sizes. Add to these, high-low shoes, which had never been acquainted with Day and Martin, held to the foot by a piece of string—and you will find the portrait of one of the yeomen of Snowdon. His residence was in the valley, at one of the few white cottages that could be seen in the distance. There was no pretension to a homestead, and little or no enclosure to the few patches of land adjoining, which were under culture for oats. On the opposite side, however, there were several head of cattle, which formed a portion of his wealth. This day to Mr. William Owen was one of peculiar interest, for it was that appointed by him for selecting his sheep ; and all his family, young men and young women, boys and girls—and there were not a few who claimed kindred to him — were occupied in the difficult and laborious task of driving the sheep together to the sides of the mountain. This was an amusing scene, for the old man, with his hands in his pockets, acted as general, now calling out with stentorian tongue to a daughter, a true picture of an Amazon, with ' Now, Bet ; now, Sian l' (Jane) ; then to a son, causing the welkin to resound again with his commands. At length, after great toil, the wild animals were got together in some-thing like a huddle.

" The temperature in the valley we had left was scorching hot ;

but here it was cold, and we had a smart fall of hail, which lasted
for some minutes. Mr. Owen told us that last spring, about
March, the winter was so severe that he lost several head of stock,
forty lambs, and fifty sheep, which were frozen to death. We now
came in sight of the black precipice, or nearly perpendicular rock,
called Clogwyn du yr Arddudwy, at the foot of which there is a
lake, the waters of which are blue, and which we passed a quarter
of a mile on our left." The distance from Dolbadarn to the top of
Snowdon is about four miles, or a little more. After passing the
Llyn d'er Arddu, just mentioned, the scene of another fatal accident
comes in view. A gentleman named Frodsham fell over the
rocks, having strayed from his party along a path to the right.
This sad event took place in August, 1859. Magnificent views are
now to be had on all sides, and shortly before reaching the summit
this path is joined by that from Capel Curig.

This is the longest and most difficult route, the distance being
nine miles, of which half at least is along a turnpike road. The
climbing begins when Gorphwysfa is reached. Soon afterwards
the fine scenery surrounding Llyn Llydaw, described above,
comes into view. The whole track from the lake to another and
smaller lake or tarn at a higher level, Llyn Glas, is most strikingly
beautiful. Immediately above the last-named tarn towers the
central peak of Snowdon—Moel-y-Wyddfa, or the "Conspicuous."

A notice of the route from Beddgelert will be found in our
account of that place.

The writer of Murray's *Guide* thus speaks of the summit :—

"The visitor who has thus arrived at the peak of Snowdon by
any of these routes will be much mistaken if he comes prepared for

mountain solitude, for Moel-y-Wyddfa in the season is one of the most crowded spots in Wales. The guides have erected two huts on the highest point, where comestibles, such as eggs and bacon, may be obtained at tolerably reasonable prices, considering the labour of getting them up. In foggy or wet weather it is no slight relief to find a dry room and blazing fire. A charge of five shillings is made for bed and breakfast, to those who wish to see the sun rise. There is no doubt that the presence of a host of excursionists is not always grateful to the lover of nature, but he must take it as it is, with all the pleasures and all the annoyances. Fortunate are they who have ascended on a cloudless day, for the prospect is one of almost boundless magnificence."

He thus sums up the view :—

" The distant views embrace the mountains of Cumberland, Westmoreland, and Lancashire, Penyghent and Ingleborough in Yorkshire, the Isle of Man, the hills of Wicklow, with a good part of the Irish coast ; while nearer home we have the whole of Anglesea and Caernarvonshire at the feet, and we might almost say the whole of North Wales. To the north and north-east rise Moel Eilio, Mynydd Mawr, the Glyders, Moel Siabod, Trifaen, Carnedds Davydd and Llewelyn, Penmaenmawr, and the Menai Straits, with the Clwydian hills in the distance. To the west are Moel Hebog, the pools of Nantllef, Drws-y-coed, Gyrngoch, and Yr Eifl, with the sparkling sea beyond ; while to the south the eye wanders over a perfect wilderness of mountains—Moelwyn, Cynicht, Moel Lledr, and the Manods above Ffestiniog ; the Arenigs, the Berwyns, Aran Benllyn and Aran Mowddy near Bala, Llawlech and the Rhinogs over Harlech, Cader Idris near Dolgelley, the rounded hills of Montgomeryshire, with Plinlymmon and the Cardiganshire hills in the far distance. Directly at the feet lie Llanberis, with its lakes, Llyn Cwellyn and Llyn-y-gader, and the beautiful vale of Nant Gwynant, while a stone might be thrown into any of the deep valleys underneath. From twenty-five to thirty lakes are visible altogether from the summit.

> " Amidst the vast horizon's stretch,
> In restless gaze the eye of wonder darts
> O'er the expanse ; mountains on mountains piled,
> And winding bays and promontories huge,
> Lakes and meandering rivers, from their source,
> Traced to the distant ocean."

Pennant gives the following account of his visit to the summit in the latter part of the last century :—

"The mountain from hence seems propped by four vast buttresses, between which are four deep cwms, or hollows : each, excepting one, has one or more lakes lodged in its distant bottom. The nearest was Ffynnon Las, or the Green Well, lying immediately below us : one of the company had the curiosity to descend a very bad way to a jutting rock, that impended over the monstrous precipice ; and he seemed like Mercury ready to take his flight from the summit of Atlas. The waters of Ffynnon Las, from this height, appeared black and unfathomable, and the edges quite green. From thence is a succession of bottoms, surrounded by lofty and rugged hills, the greatest part of whose sides are perfectly mural, and form the most magnificent amphitheatre in nature. The Wyddfa is on one side ; Crib-y-distill, with its serrated tops, on another ; Crib Goch, a ridge of fiery redness, appears beneath the preceding; and opposite to it is the boundary called Lliwedd. Another very singular support to this mountain is Y Clawdd Goch, rising into a sharp ridge, so narrow, as not to afford breadth even for a path.

" The view from this exalted situation is unbounded. In a former tour, I saw from it the county of Chester, the high hills of Yorkshire, part of the north of England, Scotland, and Ireland ; a plain view of the Isle of Man ; and that of Anglesea lay extended like a map beneath me, with every rill visible. I took much pains to see this prospect to advantage—sat up at a farm on the west till about twelve, and walked up the whole way. The night was remarkably fine and starry : towards morn, the stars faded away, and left a short interval of darkness, which was soon dispersed by the dawn of day. The body of the sun appeared more distinct, with the rotundity of the moon, before it rose high enough to render its beams too brilliant for our sight. The sea which bounded the western part was gilt by its rays, first in slender streaks, at length glowing with redness. The prospect was disclosed like the gradual drawing up of a curtain in a theatre. We saw more and more, till the heat became so powerful as to attract the mists from the various lakes, which, in a slight degree, obscured the prospect. The shadow of the mountain was flung many miles, and shewed its bicapitated form ; the Wyddfa making one, the Crib-y-distill the other head. I counted this time between twenty and thirty lakes, either in this county, or Meirioneddshire. The day proved so excessively hot, that my journey cost me the skin of the lower part of my face, before I reached the resting-place, after the fatigue of the morning.

" On this day, the sky was obscured very soon after I got up. A vast mist enveloped the whole circuit of the mountain. The prospect down was horrible. It gave an idea of numbers of abysses, concealed by a thick smoke, furiously circulating around us. Very often a gust of wind formed an opening in the clouds, which gave a fine and distinct vista of lake and valley. Sometimes they opened only in one place ; at others, in many at once, exhibiting a most strange and perplexing sight of water, fields, rocks, or chasms, in fifty different places. They then closed at once, and left us involved in darkness ; in a small time they would separate again, and fly in wild eddies round the middle of the mountains, and expose, in parts, both tops and bases clear to our view. We descended from this various scene with great reluctance."

Bingley, another old writer, in his account of North Wales, is moved to poetry by the marvels of the view. He says :—

" The view from the summit I found beyond my expectation extensive. From this point the eye is able to trace, on a clear day, part of the coast, with the hills of Scotland ; the high mountains of Westmoreland and Cumberland ; and, on this side, some of the hills of Lancashire. When the atmosphere is very transparent, even part of the county of Wicklow, and the whole of the Isle of Man, become visible. The immediately surrounding mountains of Caernarvonshire and Merionethshire all seem directly under the eye, and the highest of the whole appear from this station much lower than Snowdon. Many of the vales were exposed to the view, which, by their verdure, relieved the eye from the dreary scene of barren rocks. The numerous pools visible from hence, betwixt thirty and forty, lend also a varied character to the prospect. The mountain itself, from the summit, seems as it were propped by five immense rocks as buttresses. These are Crib-y-distill and Crib Goch, between Llanberis and Capel Curig; Lliewedd, towards Nan Hwynan; Clawdd Goch, towards Beddgelert; and Lechog, the mountain which forms the south side of the vale of Llanberis, towards Dolbadarn.

"The summit of Snowdon is so frequently enveloped in clouds and mist, that, except when the weather is perfectly fine and settled, the traveller through this country will find it somewhat difficult to have a day sufficiently clear to permit him to ascend the mountain. When the wind blows from the west, it is almost always completely covered; and at other times, even when the state of the weather seems favourable, it will often become suddenly enveloped, and will remain in that state for hours. Most persons, however, agree that the prospects are the more interesting, as they are more varied, when the clouds just cover the summit. The following description of the scenery from Snowdon when the mountain is in this state is perfectly accurate : –

> " 'Now high and swift flits the thin rack along
> Skirted with rainbow dyes, now deep below
> (While the fierce sun strikes the illumined top
> Slow sails the gloomy storm, and all beneath
> By vaporous exhalation hid, lies lost
> In darkness ; save at once where drifted mists
> Cut by strong gusts of eddying winds, expose
> The transitory scene.
> Now swift on either side the gathered clouds,
> As by a sudden touch of magic, wide

Recede, and the fair face of heaven and earth
Appears. Amid the vast horizon's stretch,
In restless gaze the eye of wonder darts
O'er the expanse ; mountains on mountains piled,
And winding bays, and promontories huge,
Lakes and meandering rivers, from their source
Traced to the distant ocean.' "

But Snowdon has not wanted for real poets. To the present
day the natives will tell us that " whoever sleeps a night upon the
top of Snowdon, will wake up as much inspired as those who
became poets by taking a nap on the hill of Apollo.

" 'Here, too, the bards, when merit claimed the meed,
The strain that gave to other days the deed,
Invoked the *Hill*, the verse-inspiring spring,
And quitted earth on rapture's rising wing ;
E'en now, unknown to cultivating care,
Some *genial plant* may feel this chilling air ;
May bud, unseen, the village oak beneath,
Or bloom, unheeded, on the barren heath :
And though its tints depression's mists may shroud,
Some beam may yet pervade th' incumbent cloud,
Some friendly hand its glowing dyes may spread,
And shew its bloom on Flora's gayest bed.' "

Lloyd.

And Evans offers the following piece of fine writing in prose as
a description of a descent into the vale of Llanberis, and
elucidatory of the mountain's poet-making powers :—" Occasional
gusts of wind which now roared around us swept away the pitchy
cloud that involved particular spots of the mountain, and discovered immediately below us huge rocks, abrupt precipices, and

profound hollows, exciting emotions of astonishment and awe in the mind, which the eye, darting down an immense descent of vacuity and horror, conveyed to it under the dreadful image of inevitable destruction."

A modern writer gives us a description of sunrise from Snowdon with a very different kind of imagery. He tells exactly what he felt and saw, and his account is therefore better, even for poetical purposes, than the long words and piled-up imagery which Evans admired:—"On reaching the summit, all our difficulties were forgotten, and our imaginary complaints overborne with exclamations of wonder, surprise, and admiration. The light, thin, misty cloud, which had for some time enveloped us, as if by enchantment, suddenly dispersed; the whole ocean appeared illuminated by a fiery substance, and all the subject hills below us— for they resembled molehills—were gradually tinged by the rich glow of the sun; whose orb becoming at length distinctly visible, displayed the whole island of Anglesea so distinctly, that we descried, as in a map, its flat and uncultivated plains, bounded by the rich and inexhaustible Parys mountains, in the vicinity of Holyhead. The point on which we were standing did not exceed a square of five yards, and we sickened almost at the sight of the steep precipices which environed us. Round it is a small parapet, formed by the customary tribute of all strangers who visit this summit, and to which we likewise contributed, by placing a large stone on its top. This parapet, indeed, sheltered us from the chilly cold, and protected us from the piercing wind, to which this height must naturally be exposed.

" We remained in this situation for a considerable time, and endeavoured, without success, to enumerate the several lakes, forests, woods, and counties, which were exposed to us in one view ; but lost and confounded with the innumerable objects worthy of admiration, and regardless of the chilling cold, we took a distinct survey of the Isle of Man, together with a faint prospect of the Highlands in Ireland, which appeared just visibly skirting the distant horizon. But another object soon engrossed all our attention :

'The wide, the unbounded prospect lay before us :
But shadows, clouds, and darkness rest upon it ;'

for we unexpectedly observed long billows of vapour tossing about, half-way down the mountain, totally excluding the country below, and occasionally dispersing, and partially revealing its features ; while above, the azure expanse of the heavens remained unobscured by the thinnest mist. This, however, was of no long continuance : a thick cloud presently wet us through ; and the point on which we were standing could alone be distinguished. As there appeared little or no chance of the clouds dispersing, we soon commenced our descent. Respecting this Alpine excursion, suffice it to say that, though our expectations were raised exceedingly high, it infinitely surpassed all conception, and baffled all description ; for no colour of language can paint the grandeur of the rising sun, observed from this eminence, or describe the lakes, woods, and forests which are extended before you ; for description, though it enumerates their names, yet it cannot draw the elegance of outline, cannot give the effect of precipices, or delineate the minute features, which reward the actual observer at every new choice of his position ; and, by changing their colour and form in his gradual ascent, till at last every object dwindles into atoms ; in short, this interesting excursion, which comprehends every thing that is awful, grand, and sublime, producing the most pleasing sensations, has left traces in the memory which the imagination will ever hold dear."

CADER IDRIS.

CADER IDRIS owes its rank and the estimation in which it is held by all lovers of scenery not so much to its height, which falls short of that of Snowdon, as to its situation at the head of a short range, and to its peculiarly precipitous slope. The highest point is two thousand nine hundred and fourteen feet above the sea ; being exceeded by half-a-dozen mountains of the rival range, and being about six hundred feet lower than Snowdon. The number of beautiful excursions which may be made in its neighbourhood, too, render it a point of universal attraction. Dolgelly, Cymmer Abbey, Nannau, the Falls of the Cain, are all to the north, and within a few miles ; while to the south are Machynlleth, with its Parliament House, and all the valleys which, one by one, unite in the Dovey, with Plinlimmon in the distance— "Proud Plinlimmon," whose cloud-capped head, as Gray tells us, bowed at the magic song of Modred.

It is from Dolgelly that visitors generally approach Cader Idris. The name is derived from Idris, a famous giant, whose chair of state was on the summit—at least so the popular legend runs ; but other, and perhaps better, explanations have been offered. The name of Dolgelly—or Dolgellen, as Evans gave it—is less puzzling. *Dol* or *Dal* is a word we have as " dale," and the remaining syllables indicate the presence in the valley of a grove of hazel trees. It has little of interest in its modern streets. The church, with its pewless floor and one old monument, and the house called the Parliament House, from a tradition that in it Owen Glendower held his parliament in 1404, are all the remnants of antiquity that the place contains. The house, however, looks much too modern to have been standing at the beginning of the fifteenth century, but it may possibly be on the site of the veritable " St. Stephen's" of North Wales. It was not here, but at Machynlleth, that Owen was crowned in 1402 ; and the porch of the Parliament House there has greater appearance of authenticity. But the greatest feature of interest—and, indeed, in a sense, of antiquity—about Dolgelly consists of its walls. It is situated so completely in the heart of the hills, that Cader Idris and its companions may be considered its fortifications. The saying is as old as the time of Fuller, and admirably sums up the peculiarity of the place.

Fuller is not content with this notice, but adds four other things worthy of remark respecting Dolgelly. His words are as follows:—

" 1. The walls thereof are three miles high.
2. Men go into it over the water ; but
3. Go out of it under the water.
4. The steeple thereof doth grow therein.
5. There are more alehouses than houses."

These enigmas he solves in the following manner :—The first alludes

to the fact that mountains surround the place. The second, that
on one entrance to the town, there was a bridge over which all
travellers must pass. The third, that on the other they had to go
under a wooden trough, carried across the road for the conveyance
of water from a distance to an overshot mill on the opposite side.
For the explanation of the fourth, that the bells (if plural) hung in
a yew tree. And fifthly, that "the tenements were divided into
two or more tippling-houses, and that even chimneyless barns were
often used for that purpose." It must be presumed that he penned
this description from the state of the town during the time of fair,
when almost every house was open for the sale of *Cwrw dda*, or
Welsh ale. Respecting the other allusions, none will at present
apply, except the first two.

Two miles from Dolgelly, the traveller, bent on ascending the
mountain, reaches the beautiful lake of Llyn Gwernan. A little
further on is Llyn-y-Gafr, and a short but steep ascent brings us to
Llyn-y-Gader—a deep and lovely tarn, high up the side of the hill,
in a magnificent amphitheatre of cliffs. Cader Idris, indeed, is well
supplied with water in which to cast reflections. At the other side
is Tal-y-Llyn, the most famous of all—perhaps the best known
and oftenest praised lake in Wales. The author of *Murray's
Guide* dwells at some length upon its merits :—"This is considered
by many the most charming lake in Wales, although in point of
size it is exceeded by several. It is but a mile and a quarter
long and a quarter of a mile broad, being, in fact, 'an expansion of
the narrow vale ; the waters from the surrounding mountains being
confined and dammed up at the lower extremity, where they run off
in a rapid stream at Penybont, under a new bridge, erected a few

years ago.'—*Notes of an Angler.* The lake is celebrated for the
rapid growth and the amazing fecundity of its trout, and is, therefore,
as a matter of course, flogged from morning to night. The depth
in general is not great, and the bottom is covered with moss and
weeds, which is the principal cause of the fish thriving so well.
The shallow weedy bottoms are the most likely spots to afford good
sport, particularly at the lower end of the lake. May and June are
the best months, and close to the village of Tal-y-Llyn is the little inn
of Tyn-y-Cornel, a comfortable and unpretending hostelry in much
repute among anglers. There is a second inn at Minffordd, at the
junction of the Dolgelly and Machynlleth roads; but it is not so
convenient, on account of the distance from the lake. A little
below Minffordd a small stream runs in from Llyn-y-Cae. The
best way of visiting this glorious tarn is by following the course
of the brook about a mile and a-half. The only lake to compare
with it in North Wales is Llyn Idwal. It lies in a very deep
hollow, surrounded on all sides but the outlet by the intensely
rugged and steep precipices of Cader Idris—

> "On every side now rose
> Rocks, which in unimaginable forms
> Lifted their black and barren pinnacles
> In the light of evening, and its precipice,
> Obscuring ravine, disclosed above
> 'Mid toppling storms."—*Shelley.*

The lake is of small size, but is all the more striking on that
account: its depth is so great (360 feet) that some have supposed it
to be the crater of an extinct volcano. Trout are abundant, of
better quality than those in Tal-y-Llyn; but the lake is little fished,
on account of the difficult walking to get to it."

Evans also praises Tal-y-Llyn, but hardly with such super-
lative adjectives as some later writers. He says of it, that though
confined, the vale is not destitute of beauty, consisting of
rich meadows "through which meanders a fine rivulet, issuing
from the lake, that soon has its confluence with the ocean.
The valley is flanked by lofty mountains, whose declivous sides
are adorned with verdant and sylvan clothing. The termination is highly picturesque. The lake here nearly fills the
valley, so as to leave only a road on one side, and then contracts
gradually into the form of a river, rushing under a bridge of one
arch, through a narrow defile, on one side of which stands the
church, and on the other cottages, intermingled with trees." This
simple and quaint description shows how taste has altered in such
matters. Wilson, the master who may be said to have first perceived the beauty of our hills and lakes, and to have ventured to
paint them as he saw them, was born not far from the foot of Cader
Idris, and lies buried close by at Mold. He is remembered in his
own country not so much by his immortal landscapes, as by the
signboard of an inn (the Three Loggerheads) which he painted.
Two figures only appear, but the inquisitive traveller is advised to
guess silently as to the identity of the third, as the consequences of
asking information are not always agreable. But Wilson could
paint better things than signboards; and if ever an artist was born
in an appropriate neighbourhood, it was he.

Continuing our ascent from Dolgelly, we cannot do better than
follow the guidance of Aikin, who, in his *Journal*, thus describes
the scene :—

"We quitted the road and began our ascent at the first step of this lofty mountain. When we had surmounted the exterior ridge, we descended a little to a deep, clear lake, which is kept constantly full by the numerous tributary torrents that fall down the surrounding rocks; hence we climbed a second and still higher chain up a steep but not difficult track, over numerous fragments of rock detached from the higher parts. We now came to a second and more elevated lake, clear as glass, and overlooked by steep cliffs in such a manner as to resemble the crater of a volcano, of which a most accurate representation is to be seen in Wilson's excellent view of Cader Idris. Some travellers have mentioned the finding lava and other volcanic productions here; upon a strict examination, however, we were unable to discover anything of the kind, nor did the water of the lake appear to differ in any respect from the purest rock water, though it was tried repeatedly with the most delicate chemical tests. A clear, loud, and distant echo repeats every shock that is made near the lake. We now began our last and most diffi-cult ascent up the summit of Cader Idris itself, which, when we had surmounted, we came to a small plain with two rocky heads of nearly equal heights, one looking to the north, and the other to the south : we made choice of that which appeared to us the most elevated, and seated ourselves on its highest pinnacle to rest, after a laborious ascent of three hours. We were now high above all the eminences within this vast expanse, and as the clouds gradually cleared away, caught some grand views of the surrounding country. The huge rocks which we before looked up to with astonishment, were far below at our feet, and many a small lake appeared in the valleys between them ; to the north, Snowdon, with its dependencies, shut up the scene ; on the west, we saw the whole curve of the bay of Cardigan, bounded at a vast distance by the Caernarvon mountains; and nearer, dashing its white breakers against the rocky coasts of Merioneth, the southern horizon was bounded by Plinlimmon, and at the east, the eye glanced over the lake of Bala, the two Arenig mountains, the two Arrans, the long chain of the Ferwyn mountains, to the Breiddin hills on the confines of Shropshire ; and dimly, in the distant horizon, was beheld the Wrekin, rising alone from the plain of Salop. Having at last satisfied our curiosity, and being thoroughly chilled by the keen air of these elevated regions, we began to descend the side opposite to that which we had come up. The first stage led us to another beautiful mountain lake, whose cold clear waters discharge their superabundance in a full stream down the side of the mountain. All these waters abound with trout, and in some is found the gwyniad, a fish particular to rocky Alpine lakes. Following the course of the stream, we came on the edge of the craggy cliffs that overlook Tal-y-Llyn lake ; and a long and difficult descent conducted us at last on the borders of Tal-y-Llyn, where we entered the Dolgelly road."

Another traveller thus describes this view (Warner's *First Walk through Wales*) :—

" The afternoon was gloriously fine, and the atmosphere perfectly clear, so that the vast unbounded prospect lay beneath, unobscured by cloud, vapour, or any other interruption, to the astonished and delighted eye, which threw its glance over a varied scene, including a circumference of at least five hundred miles. To the north-east was Ireland, like a distant mist upon the ocean ; and a little to the right was Snowdon, and the other mountains of Caernarvonshire. Further on, in the same direction, the Isle of

Man, the neighbourhood of Chester, Wrexham, and Salop; the sharp head of the Wrekin, and the undulating summit of the Cleehills. To the south, I saw the country round Clifton, Pembrokeshire, St. David's, and Swansea; to the west, a vast prospect of the British Channel, bounded by the horizon. Exclusive of these distant objects, the nearer views were wonderfully striking. Numberless mountains, of different forms, appearances, and elevation, rose in all directions; which, with the various harbours, lakes, and rivers, towns, villages, and villas, scattered over the extensive prospect, combined to form a scene inexpressibly august, diversified, and impressive."

Mr. Bingley ascended this mountain from the Blue Lion, an inn kept in his day by the guide. From this spot Mr. Bingley declares himself capable of attaining the summit in two hours, from which he describes the views to be more varied than those from Snowdon, if not so extensive.

" In descending," he says, " I took a direction eastward of that in which I had gone up, and proceeded along that part of the mountain called Mynydd Moel. The path in this direction is sufficiently sloping to allow a person to ride even to the summit. A gentleman, mounted on a little Welsh pony, had done this a few days before I was here."

Some years ago, a Cheshire lady rode a pony right over Cader Idris, from Dolgelly to Minffordd. Her steed, it need hardly be added, was a native.

Most visitors will cross the river to Cymmer Abbey, a Cistercian house, situated, as usual with that order, in the midst of most beautiful natural scenery. It is called by olden writers, and also by the people of the neighbourhood, Vanner Abbey. The name Cymmer is Welsh, and signifies the "meeting of the waters." The church, as usual in the English Cistercian buildings, is of the severe style which marked the first introduction of the pointed arch. The east end is almost covered with ivy. A more lovely spot than this for the purpose can hardly be conceived ; and the enthusiastic tourist may be excused who thinks that ruins are much better than complete buildings, and that the final cause of Cistercian abbeys was to beautify such places as Tintern or Studley or Cymmer. The founders were Meredith and Griffith ap Conan, late in the twelfth century ; and the chief benefactor was Llewelyn ap Jorwerth, of whom we have spoken in our notice of Bethgelert. The abbot's house, now the residence of a farmer, is of the fifteenth or six-teenth century, and has a hall with an old oak roof. The history of Cymmer was not uneventful, and has been thus summed up :—

"About thirty years subsequent to the supposed period of its foundation, it appears to have been in a flourishing state ; but the evils arising out of war, more especially those which visit the seat of warfare, soon cast a paralysing damp on its rising prosperity. When Henry the Third was marching a formidable army against the Welsh, who had asserted their independence under their intre-pid leader, Prince Llewelyn ap Jorwerth, and invested Montgomery Castle, a monk of this house, happening to be on a service of espion-age, was strictly examined as to the situation and strength of the Cambrian forces. Naturally considering it a duty incumbent upon every man possessed of patriotism to befriend his own country rather than assist an enemy, he gave an exaggerated account of the opposing army, and misrepresented their different positions. The

Welsh made a *ruse de guerre*, feigning a retreat to an extensive marsh, not far distant from the site of the first onset, on which the English troops eagerly pursued what they conceived to be the vanquished enemy ; but being encumbered with heavy armour, and still further annoyed by the treacherous nature of the ground, they were unable to act offensively, or even retreat, before the light active troops to which they were opposed returned to the charge ; and after a short conflict, victory decided in favour of the Welsh. The King, incensed at the deception, and enraged by the sanguinary as well as disastrous consequences that ensued, on passing by the religious house to which the informer belonged, gave command for its destruction by fire.   All the out offices were consumed in the conflagration ; but the abbot, having expurgated himself and the resident brethren from any privacy of the transaction, after profound submission, earnest entreaties, and subjecting the estates to a fine of three hundred marks, saved the rest of the building.   At the dissolution, the annual revenues were estimated, according to Speed's valuation, at £58 15s., or about £600 a-year in modern money."

CONWAY CASTLE.

THE river Conway—or, as it is often and perhaps more correctly spelt, Conwy—falls into the sea at a place as nearly as possible half-way between Chester and Holyhead. The English city is forty-five miles to the east, the Welsh port forty to the west. The river at high water is about half-a-mile across; and before 1826, it could only be crossed by a ferry. In 1806 the mails between London and Ireland were lost by the swamping of the ferry-boat, and all the passengers but two were drowned. Many were the contrivances proposed for bridging this dangerous gulf. The tide ran with violence, and the banks were shelving near the water's edge. At length Telford, then engaged making the great Holyhead road, succeeded in crossing it with a suspension bridge, upwards of a hundred yards in length, and connected by vast embankments with the upper shores. On the western side of the river stands the mighty castle, which Edward the First began in 1284, and which was built by the same great architect (Henry de Elreton) who also designed Caernarvon. If he had intended Conway for picturesque beauty alone, he could not have succeeded better. It is regular in plan, and full of symmetry. It appears to grow, as if by nature, out of the cliff which it crowns; and age, which has denuded it of its strength, has added tenfold to its picturesqueness. But although beauty was by no means left out of the question in a building which was to be as much a palace as a castle, strength was Elreton's first and chief object. He took care that his work should be perfect as a fortress, and left its appearance to take care of itself; thus carrying out to the utmost a cardinal principle of mediæval architecture. The result, now that the softening influences of time have been at work upon it for nearly six centuries, shows how sound the principle was. The use of Conway Castle has departed; its beauty is greater than ever.

Mr. Hartshorne, whose account of Caernarvon we shall find very useful when speaking of that castle, has only touched incidentally on Conway. But from what he tells us, it seems that Edward and his Queen visited it several times, and on one occasion spent their Christmas within its walls. Perhaps it was at this time that the wild Welsh came down from their mountain fastnesses, and besieged the King and his court so closely, that for some days they were in danger of starvation, but were relieved at length by a fleet.

During the fourteenth century we hear little of Conway, or Aberconway, as it is sometimes called. But in the last year of that century it emerges from obscurity, and comes prominently forward in history. Henry of Bolingbroke, Duke of Lancaster, the son of John of Gaunt, having been banished from England by Richard the Second ten years before, had returned while Richard was in Ireland,

and had been joined by all those whom the King had alienated by his tyrannical government. Even the Duke of York, the next heir by right to the throne, espoused Henry's cause; and Richard, hastening over by Milford Haven, marched but a short way towards his enemy, when, suspecting the fidelity of his soldiers, he deserted them at night, with thirteen companions, and fled to Conway. Froissart describes this flight with his usual graphic touch; but, being ignorant of Welsh geography, he speaks of Flint where he ought to have said Conway. The following passage contains the climax of the story :—

"When matters could not longer be concealed, it was told to King Richard—'Sire, take care of yourself; you must have good and speedy counsel, for the Londoners have risen with a mighty power, and intend to march against you. They have elected the Earl of Derby (Duke of Lancaster), your cousin, their commander; and by his advice they act. You may be assured that some strong treaties have been entered into between them, since he has crossed the sea by their invitation.' The King was thunderstruck at hearing this, and knew not what answer to make, for his courage forsook him, and he foresaw affairs would end badly unless proper steps were immediately taken. Having mused a while, he replied to the knights who had given him this information—' Instantly make ready our men-at-arms and archers, and issue a special summons throughout the kingdom for the assembling of all my vassals, as I will not fly before my subjects.' ' By God,' answered the knights, ' everything goes badly, for your men are leaving you and running off. You have already lost half your army, and the remainder are panic-struck and wavering.' ' What can I do, then ?' asked the King.

'We will tell you, sire; quit the field, for you cannot hold it longer, and make for one of your castles, where you can remain until your step-brother, Sir John Holland, who is enterprising and courageous, and must now have heard of the rebellion, come to you. He will, by force or negotiations, bring your affairs into a different state from that in which they are at present. When it is known that he has taken the field, many who have fled from you will join him.' The King agreed to the advice. The Earl of Salisbury was not then with him, but in another part of the country; and, when he heard that the Earl of Derby was marching a large army against the King, he judged things would turn out badly for his master and for all who had been his advisers. He therefore remained quiet, waiting for further intelligence.

"The Duke of York had not accompanied the King on this expedition; but his son, the Earl of Rutland, had been induced to join him for two reasons—one, in return for the great affection King Richard had shown him; the other, because he was Constable of England. It was therefore necessary he should attend his King. Other news was brought the King as he supped. They said— 'Sire, you must determine how you will act; for your army is as nothing compared to the force marching against you, and a combat will be of no avail; and appease the malcontents as you have formerly done, by kind words and fair promises, and punish them afterwards at your leisure. There is a castle twelve miles from hence, called Flint (Conway), that is tolerably strong; we therefore advise that you fly thither, and remain shut up as long as you please, or until you hear other news from Sir John Holland and your friends. We will send to Ireland for succour; and when the

King of France, your father-in-law, shall hear of your distress, he
will assist you.' King Richard listened to this advice, and thought
it good. He selected such as he wished to accompany him, and
ordered the Earl of Rutland to remain at Bristol with the remnant
of the army, ready prepared to advance when they should hear
other news, or when they should be sufficiently strong to combat
their enemies. These commands were obeyed; and the King, attended by his household only, departed on the ensuing morning for
Flint Castle (Conway), which they entered without showing any
appearance of making war on anyone, but solely to defend themselves and the place should they be attacked."

A French metrical chronicler says that it was break of day
when he arrived at Conway, which is called a place " where
the houses are covered with tiles." There he found the Earl
of Salisbury. "At the meeting of the King and the earl,
instead of joy, there was very great sorrow. Tears, lamenta-
tions, sighs, groans, and mourning quickly broke forth. Truly it
was a piteous sight to behold their looks and countenance and
woful meeting." The earl's face was pale with watching; he
related to the King his hard fate, and how he had made his muster,
and described the impossibility of obtaining men willing to fight
against the duke. Richard, we are told, received this intelligence
with many ejaculations of grief. "No one would believe," says the
quaint rhymer, "how much the King grieved at it." He continued
some time at Conway, "where he had no more with him than two
or three of his intimate friends, sad and distressed. . . . Every
one was very uneasy for himself with sufficient cause. Reckoning
nobles and other persons, we were but sixteen in all." The

chronicler here bursts forth into a long tirade against the fickleness
of fortune; at last very sensibly resolving, "I shall here at present
speak no more of fortune, for a prudent man would take no notice
of her benefits, but in a reasonable way. I shall now come to the
conclusion of King Richard, who, from sport of fortune together
with treason, as I have already said, was all alone at Conway, full
of sorrow, mourning, and dismay. I know full well that he and the
earl said it would be a great thing to send to his people, whom he had
lately left at the seaport, Milford Haven, to come thither without
delay." But a horseman arrived, who told them of the defection of
the army Richard had left. When this bearer of evil tidings had
finished his narrative, the King again breaks out into imprecations
and prayers; and, if the chronicler may be trusted, his conduct was
far from dignified. He invoked the judgments of heaven on the
deserters in a long speech, concluding, "For well I know that when
the latter day shall come, and He shall hold His judgment, the
wicked shall neither have refuge nor reprieve, but shall find what
they have done and spoken; and then shall they be accursed from
His mouth, as we are told, in pain infernal. Such is our belief.
Wherefore, in every respect we take heed unto ourselves; and this
it is often said, power hath no law." Then said the earl, "Sire, by
my honour, you speak the truth." They then agreed to make no
farther stay at Conway, for they were greatly afraid, and with good
reason. They went straight to Beaumaris, which was ten miles
from Conway.

Beaumaris, which was one of the castles built by Edward the
First, was usually considered impregnable in that age; but Richard
did not remain there long, he went back again to Caernarvon; every-

where he lamented his fate, which he had brought upon himself, in most unmanly and bitter language. "There was not a man," says the chronicler, "so hard-hearted or so firm, who would not have wept at the sight of the disgrace that was brought upon him."

It would be interesting to know the name of the writer to whom we are indebted for this curious narrative. Strutt cites him as Francis de la Marque. But he does so by a mistranslation of the words of the title of his metrical history, where he is described as a French gentleman of distinction, *un gentilhomme Francois de marque.* He accompanied a certain knight, his friend; and the two seem to have been sent by the French king (Richard's father-in-law) to be present in the Irish war. His account is very impartial, but he seems to have acquired a personal regard for the King, and attended him until his deposition. His metrical history of this event was printed in full in the twentieth volume of the *Archæologia,* 1824, under the direction of the Rev. John Webb. The fate of Richard the Second was accounted one of the most interesting of stories, and in addition to an immense number of more or less romantic histories of it which are still extant in manuscript, we have Shakespeare's famous play.

At Caernarvon, Richard was poorly lodged in the castle. It was not customary, except in time of necessity, to keep these expensive fortresses in any high state of repair; and when the court moved from one to another, large quantities of tapestry, furniture, and even glass for the windows, was carried about with the suite. So we are not surprised to read that "in his castles to which he retired there was no furniture, nor had he anything to lie down upon but straw; really he lay in this manner for four or six nights, for in truth not a farthing's worth of victuals, or of anything else, was to be found in them. Certes, I dare not tell the great misery of the king, who stayed not long at Caernarvon, for he had little rest then on account of his misfortune and great poverty. He returned to Conway, where he thus greatly bewailed his wife :—'My mistress and my consort! accursed be the man—little doth he love us—who thus shamefully separateth us two!'" There are several lines of this lamentation, which seems strange to us, considering that at this time Richard was thirty years of age, and a widower, who had only been married in form to a child of eleven, who was being brought up at Windsor to be his wife. She was eventually sent back to France, and married to the eldest son of the Duke of Orleans. Her younger sister, Catherine, was, many years later, the wife of Henry the Fifth, the son and successor of this very Duke of Lancaster from whom Richard was now a fugitive.

At last a messenger was sent to Henry, who detained him, and sent the Earl of Northumberland to take the King. He was at Conway still, "in sorrow and dismay ;" he knew nothing of the coming of the earl, but he often said, "I cannot tell what this can mean. . . . What can have become of my brother-in-law of Exeter ? it is eight days since he went to Chester, to bring the duke and me to an agreement." Northumberland meanwhile was engaged in arrangements for securing the King's person, feeling sure that if he was aware of their strength he would not leave the walls of his castle. The following passage so well describes the situation of Conway, that we must quote it almost entire :—"He formed his men into two bodies, under the rough and lofty cliffs of a rock ; they were fresh, and eager—persecuting traitors as they were—to

take the King. . . . The subtle earl said to his people, "Keep
well this pass. I am going over, with five others, to the opposite
shore. . . . Ere to-morrow's dawn, I will, in prose or in rhyme,
tell the King such tidings as, unless he be harder than file of
tempered steel, I think shall make him leave his quarters. But
beware that ye stir not for your lives, till you see the King or
myself return." So they put themselves in good array ; and the
earl, without making any stir, went on to Conway to fulfil his word.

There is an arm of the sea before the town ; but when the earl
came in front of it, he sent a herald to King Richard, to ask if he
would be pleased to grant him safe conduct, that he might pass
over to tell him how the duke was desirous of coming to an
agreement with him. Then the herald crossed the water, and found
the King aloft in the castle, hardly assailed by sorrow. He said
cheerfully to him, "Sire, the honourable Earl of Northumberland
hath sent me hither to relate to you how desirous Duke Henry is to
be immediately at peace with you. May it please you, for the better
knowledge of the truth, to grant him safe conduct and leave to
come here, for otherwise he will not presume to stir." Salisbury,
who was there, then said to King Richard that it would be a good
thing to make him come thither alone. Then the King said aloud
to the messenger in his own language, "I heartily give the Earl of
Northumberland permission to pass." He thanked him a hundred
times, descended from the lofty castle, and passed the water, where
the earl had been long expecting him. There he related to him
how King Richard had freely granted him safe conduct, and
besought him to make haste. Then the earl went on board a
vessel, and crossed the water. He found King Richard, and the

Earl of Salisbury with him, as well as the Bishop of Carlisle. He said to the King, "Sire, Duke Henry hath sent me hither, to the end that an agreement should be made between you, and that you should be good friends for the time to come. If it be your pleasure, sire, and I may be heard, I will deliver to you his message, and conceal nothing of the truth :—If you will be a good judge and true, and will bring up all those whom I shall here name to you, by a certain day, for the ends of justice; listen to the parliament which you shall lawfully cause to be held between you at Westminster; and restore him to be chief judge of England, as the duke (his father) and all his ancestors had been for more than a hundred years."

At length, and after much parley, Richard consented to the terms proposed by Northumberland, who, on his part, took an oath on the Sacrament, in the chapel of Conway Castle, that the intentions with which he had come were perfect, fair, straightforward, and open. On receiving this assurance, Richard started for Flint, preceded by Northumberland, who awaited him where his men had been placed in ambush. When the King and his companions had passed, they came out and cut off his retreat, making him virtually a prisoner. The rest of the story is well known ; and as it does not concern Conway Castle, we may summarise it, and refer the reader to Shakespeare and Froissart, and the numberless other writers by whom the tragical end of King Richard the Second has been narrated. He was met at Flint by Henry, who, on the 29th September, extorted from him a deed of resignation of the crown ; and, a few days later, the House of Lords decided, on the motion of the Earl of Northumberland, whose perjury and treachery we have described, that Richard should be placed in perpetual confinement in some secret place. Within six months it was reported that he had died at Pontefract; and his body, having been exhibited at St. Paul's, was buried at Langley, in Hertfordshire, but eventually removed to Westminster Abbey by Henry V., where his tomb had probably been made in his lifetime, and where the curious epitaph is still to be seen :—" Obruit hereticos—et eorum stravit amicos" (he burned heretics and slaughtered their friends). In a later part of our French chronicler's work, he notices a curious prophecy regarding Conway, which, he says, was told him by an ancient knight, as they rode together towards Chester :—" He told me that Merlin and Bede had, from the time in which they lived, prophesied of the taking and ruin of the King, and that if I were in his castle he would show it me in form and manner as I had seen it come to pass, saying thus—'There shall be a king in Albion, who shall reign for the space of twenty or two-and-twenty years, in great honour and in great power, and shall be allied and united with those of Gaul, which king shall be undone in the ports of the north in a triangular place.' Thus the knight told me it was written in a book belonging to him. The triangular place he applied to the town of Conway; and for this he had a very good reason, for I can assure you that it is a triangle, as though it had been so laid down by a true and exact measurement. In the said town of Conway was the King sufficiently undone; for the Earl of Northumberland drew him forth, as you have already heard, by the treaty which he made with him; and from that time he had no power. Thus the knight held this prophecy to be true, and attached thereunto great faith and credit; for such is the nature of them in

their country, that they very thoroughly believe in prophecies,
phantoms, and witchcraft, and employ (have recourse to) them
right willingly.   Yet, in my opinion, this is not right, but is a great
want of faith."

Upon this passage Mr. Webb, the translator, makes the following
note :—" The triangular shape of the town of Conway may be well
distinguished from the small terrace or rampart at the western
entrance, which commands the whole of the walls.   Edward I., by
whom it was laid down and fortified, had his choice of the form :
it has been thought to bear reference to that of a Welsh harp ; but
this is too visionary a conjecture.   No doubt it was adapted to the
nature of the site and the exigencies of the situation.   Such was
clearly the case from the outline of it ; and I must take leave to
correct the author's assertion as to its being exactly triangular, a
little variation to the left, owing to the cast of the bank, being
visible from the point already mentioned. .   . The castle
commanded the port and passage over the river, and protected
a frequented entrance into the interior of Wales.   The position was
admirably selected, and the work capitally executed.   The masonry
of the whole of the walls is of a very superior kind as to strength
and beauty ; and much of it promises, unless disturbed by violence,
to resist the efforts of time for centuries to come.   Here Richard,
with proper precautions and a moderate force, might have felt
himself secure ; or, as a last resource, might have found means of
escaping by sea.   Conway must have been neglected, or very ill
defended, after the King was enticed out of it.   Gwilym-ap-Tudor
and Rhys (his brother) received a pardon (2 Henry IV.) for having,
with many of their people, taken the castle and burnt the town.

This fortress had been, or was afterwards, used as a prison. John Claydon, a Lollard of London, was confined in it for two years, when Braybrook, who died in 1404, was Bishop of London."

In another note, Mr. Webb says that "in the course of his inquiries, not long since, he took this metrical history, and compared it upon the spot with the castle of Conway. There he recognised the venerable arch of the eastern window of the chapel still entire, where must have stood the altar at which mass was performed when the fatal oath was taken. The chapel, in which Richard conferred with his friends, is at the eastern extremity of the hall."

The plan of the town, with the castle at one corner, does indeed resemble a harp, being three-cornered, owing not to any intention of the builder, but rather to the exigencies of the position at the extremity of a kind of promontory washed on two sides by the sea and the river.

When Richard was at Conway, he was attended by a Welsh gentleman who had long been attached to him, and who had probably been knighted a short time before. He gave evidence in the famous Scrope and Grosvenor controversy as Sir Owen de Glendore, so called from the territory of Glendwrdwy which he owned in Merioneth. He was with Richard at Flint, when he was dismissed by Henry; and, returning to his home, was eventually destined, as Owen Glendower, to lure to their destruction the Earl of Northumberland, whose base share in betraying Richard we have already seen, and his son, the more famous Henry, Lord Percy, usually known by the *nomme de guerre* of Hotspur. We have occasion to speak more at length of Glendower in another place.

We hear little or nothing of Conway for many years after this time. The civilisation of Wales was still far from having been accomplished, and no doubt a large garrison was kept in this and other castles of that turbulent country. The insurrection of Glendower, the Wars of the Roses, the many circumstances in the early life of Henry the Seventh which connected him with Wales, besides his Welsh origin and his surname of Tudor, or Theodore, all conspired to keep Conway and the other fortresses of this coast in the full stream of current events until it next emerges prominently, which was not until the great rebellion, when it fell into the custody of the warlike Archbishop Williams, himself a Welshman, and one of the last ecclesiastical dignitaries who ever held civil and military power in England. Mr. Evans thus summarises this episode in the history of Conway :—

"At the commencement of the civil wars, it was garrisoned for King Charles the First by Dr. John Williams, Archbishop of York, to whose custody numbers of the country gentlemen confided their plate and other valuables and movables, receiving a receipt from the arch-prelate, who considered himself answerable for their restoration on the return of better times. He at the same time bestowed the government of the castle on his nephew, William Hookes, in the year 1643. In May, 1645, Prince Rupert impolitically superseded the Archbishop in the command of North Wales. Irritated at this insulting conduct, it being done without the smallest attention to give him any virtual security for the property of which he had previously received the charge, Williams became decisively disgusted ; and having received an offer from Mytton of protection, under the Parliamentarian authority, he joined issue with that general, and assisted in the reduction of Conwy. The

town was taken by storm on August 15, 1646, and the castle
surrendered on the 10th of November. For these services, the
Archbishop, who had received a wound in the neck, obtained a
general pardon for his prior opposition to the Parliament, and a
release from the sequestration that had been made of his estates;
and Mytton, whose character partook more of haughtiness than
avarice, restored to every individual the property previously
entrusted to the arch-prelate's care."

Archbishop Williams deserves a longer notice than this. He
was employed in so many various capacities, that his name turns
up almost unexpectedly in half-a-dozen different and distinct places.
He was Dean of Westminster; he was Keeper of the Great Seal;
he was Bishop of Lincoln; he was a patron of art, and encouraged
the English manufacture of tapestry, among other enterprises; he
defended Conway; and his portrait occurs in one of Hollar's prints
with a gun upon his shoulder. Dean Stanley, in his *Memorials of
Westminster Abbey*, has frequent occasion to speak of him. Fuller,
in his *Worthies*, mentions that he was born at Conway, or rather,
as he writes it, at "Aber Conway;" but apparently Fuller did not
admire Williams, for he says, "I have offended his friends because I
wrote so little in his praise, and distasted his foes because I said
so much in his defence. But I had rather to live under the indig-
nation of others for relating what may offend, than die under the
accusation of my own conscience for reporting what is untrue."
Yet learning owed something to Williams, who founded the library
of Westminster Abbey. He attended the deathbed of James the
First, and preached his funeral sermon from the text, " Solomon
slept with his fathers, and he was buried in the city of David, his

father;" taking care not to read the next line, which tells of Rehoboam. Charles the First loved him not, whether for this sermon or for other reasons; and Laud was made Archbishop of Canterbury over his head. During one of the early outbreaks of fanatical fury among the Presbyterians, he defended the Abbey, "as he afterwards defended Conway Castle." He was promoted to the Archbishopric of York just before the war broke out, and followed the King to the North. His death took place a few weeks only after the execution of King Charles. He was certainly the most distinguished of the natives of Conway; but whether his distinction corresponded to any great mental or moral qualifications, we are not prepared to determine. A letter is still extant in the collection of Mr. Ormsby Gore, at Brogynton, in Shropshire, in which, under the date of July 27, 1647, King Charles, then at Ruperry, orders the goods in the castle of Aberconway to be kept safe from embezzlement, and to let the respective owners have them, they having been put in there for safety while the place was in charge of the Archbishop. This letter rather militates against the statement of Evans, quoted above, that the goods were restored by General Mytton.

But after sustaining and surviving so many shocks of war, Conway was ruined in time of peace. The Parliamentarians, though they dismantled so many other castles, spared Conway. The Commonwealth left it unmolested; and it was not until 1665, in the reign of Charles the Second, that it was dismantled. Among the Welsh retinue of Richard the Second was a certain knight, called, probably from the place of his birth, Henry Conway. His descendants were seated in Flintshire, and were successively in the service of several English monarchs. Sir Hugh was knighted by Henry the Seventh; Edward Conway was usher to Henry the Eighth; Sir John was made a banneret in the Scottish war of Edward the Sixth. The grandson of this soldier was the first Lord Conway. He had an estate in Ulster, as well as one in Warwickshire, and was made an Irish peer as Viscount Kilultagh. His son obtained from Charles the Second a grant of Conway Castle; and no sooner did he gain possession, than he ordered an agent to remove the timber, iron, lead, and other materials, under a pretence of requiring them for the King's service. It is generally understood that they were employed in repairing the buildings on his estate at Lisburn, in Ireland; and notwithstanding many remonstrances from the local authorities, the castle was unroofed, the floors removed, and what had been up to that time in fairly perfect condition reduced to a ruin. Mr. Bulkeley, Mr. Wynn, and others of rank and influence in the county, were distressed at the determination of Lord Conway, and seem, before he carried it out, to have interfered with the steward, Milward; for the following letter is extant, and was printed by Pennant (*Tours in Wales*, Vol. II., Appendix):—

" Honb¹ᵉ Friends,

        " I have had the honor to receive yoʳ letter of the 20ᵗʰ Sepᵗ, in which you are pleas'd to enquire of me whether my servant Milward doth act by my order, for the taking down of the lead, timber, and iron of Conway Castle; in answer to which question, I do by this acknowledg it to be my act and deed; and that the said Milward is employed by me to dispose of the timber and iron according to such direction as I gave him; and to transporte the lead into Ireland, where I hope it will be more serviceable to his Matie then it was in this country. And having this opportunity of addressing myselfe to you, I humbly beseech you to take off the restraint which you have put upon his proceedings, and to affoord him yor favour in it; for I am already prejudiced by the losse of shipping, and an opportune season for transportation of the lead; yet I shall esteeme this as a particular obligation upon mee, and be ready to expresse it by all the service in my power to every one of you, that you are pleased to grant this at my request, which otherwise may put me to some trouble and delay. And I doubt not of meeting occasions to testifie my being,

"Honble Sirs,

"Yo^r affectionate and obedient Servt,

"CONWAY & KILULTA.

"Ragley, in Warwickshire,
16th Oct., 1665.

"For the Honble Thomas Bulkeley, Esqr;
Colonell Wynn, Hugh Wynn, Esqr;
Thomas Vaughan, Esqr, His Ma^{tie's}
Deputy-Livetenants in North Wales."

Pennant quotes a notice of Conway in ruin from Dyer's poem of *Gronyar Hill.* The lines will describe its period of decay:—

"Deep at its feet in Conway's flood
His sides are clothed with waving wood;
And ancient towers crown his brow,
That cast an awful look below;
Whose ragged walls the ivy creeps,
And with her arms from falling keeps;

So both a safety from the wind
On mutual dependence find.
'Tis now the raven's blank abode,
'Tis now th' appartment of the toad ;
And there the fox securely feeds,
And there the poisonous adder breeds,
Concealed in ruins, moss, and weeds ;
While ever and anon there falls
Huge heaps of hoary, mouldered walls.
Yet time has seen, that lifts the low,
And level lays the lofty brow—
Has seen this broken pile complete,
Big with the vanity of state ;
But transient is the smile of Fate !
A little rule, a little sway,
A sunbeam in a winter's day,
Is all the proud and mighty have
Betwixt the cradle and the grave."

Some care is now taken of Conway Castle. It is rented by a lady, who holds it from the Crown for 6s. 8d. a-year, and the service of a basket of fish to the Queen when she passes by this way ; and something is done to arrest the progress of decay, and to preserve what remains for future ages. The tall towers overhang the railway, and appear almost to threaten it ; but though the engineers at first proposed to run their line right through the castle, no harm has come to it from this cause, and the number of people who annually visit it is greatly increased. The following brief and simple enumeration of the principal features of the ruins occurs in Murray's *Handbook to North Wales :—*

"In plan it is nearly a parallelogram, with eight drum towers 40 feet in diameter, four at the angles, and four intermediate on the north and south sides, rising nearly from the edge of the precipice, and connected with lofty curtains. In advance of the east and west ends are raised platforms, each having three low bastion or bartizan towers. From the right on the north side is a sallyport, to which access was gained by means of a river-path winding up the rock ; while on the same position on the west is the main gate, approaching over a steep drawbridge, and through a covered entrance with flanking turrets. The interior is unequally divided by a cross wall, which forms a sort of inner court marked by four of the round towers, each of which has a lofty stair turret. The principal feature in the interior is the hall of Llewelyn, on the south side, 130 feet long. It is now roofless, but was once ribbed with eight stone ribs, of which four remain ; and furnished with three fireplaces, as though intended to be converted by tapestry into several chambers. It is also lighted by nine early English windows. The vaults underneath were magazines for stores. It appears from old documents that this hall was built on account of the original one being too small. The two eastern towers are called the King's and Queen's ; and in the latter, which is the most northerly, is an oratory, a beautiful little recess in the thickness of the wall, with a polygon east end, groined. It contains seven bays, and some trefoil panels as sedilia. In the lower chamber are some curious fragments of decorated tracing. Under the King's Tower is a vault, which was accessible only through a trap-door in the floor above. On the south side is the keep, and a tower called Twrdarn or Broken Tower, the base of which has been at one time completely excavated by the irreverent inhabitants of the town, and now presents a dangerous-looking chasm, almost overhanging the railway.

The dangers of the inlet which Conway defends had long been famous before Telford succeeded in bridging the chasm. Dean Swift is said to have written some doggerel verses on the dangers of the road, and they are alluded to by Johnson. But nothing was done of much practical import till the great road of Telford was constructed, and the suspension bridge successfully designed and made. This was in 1829; and it was certainly high time something should be done. We have already spoken of the loss of a mail-boat; but Mr. Cliffe thus details the list of such casualties at Menai, which will give an idea of the perils of travel in these regions before the two suspension bridges were constructed :—

"On the 5th Dec., 1664, a boat was upset in crossing Menai Strait, and only one person was saved out of 81 passengers. His name was Hugh Williams. On the same day and month, 1785, another boat was capsized with 60 passengers, who were all drowned, with the exception of one, a Hugh Williams !! On the 5th Aug., 1820, a third boat with 25 passengers was upset, and all were drowned, excepting one, who also bore the charmed name of Hugh Williams! I I Again, on the 20th May, 1842, a boat was crossing the Menai, near the spot where the above catastrophes happened, when she upset with 15 passengers, and all perished save one; but in this instance the name of the survivor was Richard Thomas."

Mr. Cliffe says of the suspension bridge :—"The passage of the Conway at full tide is more than half-a-mile across, was formerly rather formidable to travellers, there being a very rapid tideway, and the ferrymen being most rapacious. On Christmas-day, 1806, an overloaded ferry-boat, conveying the Irish mail-coach, was upset during a heavy swell, and only two persons saved out of 15. The improvements determined on by Government in the coast Holyhead road involved the construction of the chain bridge, which was begun, on Mr. Telford's plans, in 1822, and finished in 1826. Its width, measured between the centres of the supporting towers, is 327 feet. 'The roadway is made of layers of plank, affixed by vertical bars to two sets of suspending chains, each of which contains four chains, and each chain five bars; the chains are fastened into the rock under the castle on one side, and deep into the solid rock on the island on the other.' The embankment across the sands is 2013 feet long, and is constructed of mountain clay, faced with loose stones, which have firmly withstood the most violent gales."

But fine as the suspension bridge is, it is surpassed by the tubular bridge, which Mr. Stephenson made before trying the wider passage at Menai. It "was commenced early in 1847. A steam-engine, extensive workshops, and other appliances, were erected on the river-side, a little above the castle; an immense platform was constructed on a piece of level ground that projected into the river; and the first tube was completed in about twelve months, its flotation on pontoons having been effected on Monday, March 6, 1848. Six pontoons, each 100 feet long, were used for the purpose; and as this was the first experiment of the kind, the interest was naturally intense. In a few hours the colossal gallery was warped alongside its piers. The power employed to elevate was concentrated in a couple of steam-engines, and two hydraulic rams. Only four lifts, of 6 feet each, were required at Conwy from these enormous hydraulic presses, 24 feet being the height of the bridge above the tidal level. When elevated to the required height, it at first ' dangled in the air, as though a mere plaything in the hands of the two hydraulic giants ;" and it was finally adjusted in its place on Monday, the 17th April. An engine went through on the following day.—The second tube was floated on October 12th of the same year, and finished on November 15th following. Each tube is 412 feet long, 14 feet wide, and $22\frac{1}{2}$ feet high at the ends, and weighs about 1300 tons. The height gradually increases towards the centre, a form obviously calculated to secure additional strength, as well as to prevent an accumulation of rain water : at that point it is $25\frac{1}{2}$ feet high, and galvanised iron is used for the covering throughout. These tubes have been exposed to severe tests, but the deflection has been exceedingly trifling ; and experience has proved that that which arises from the temperature does not vary up and down more than an inch."

It has been remarked, that if one of these tubes was set on end in St. Paul's Churchyard, it would reach about 12 feet above the cross on the top of the dome.

MOEL SIABOD.

LTHOUGH people who are willing to exert themselves in climbing, choose, as a rule, to attack Snowdon before they try their limbs and lungs by an ascent of Moel Siabod, it is by no means to be neglected, if for no other reason because of the magnificent view its summit affords. All views from Snowdon suffer for the absence of Snowdon itself, so conspicuous from every other mountain in the neighbourhood; but those who look from the head of Moel Siabod have the advantage of including Snowdon in their range, and more than gain in interest what they lose in elevation. Thus in many senses is it true that lookers-on see most of the game; and there are other situations in life besides the highest worthy to satisfy an ordinary ambition. Moel Siabod stands only ninth in order after Snowdon, but its situation gives it advantages which some of the greater altitudes do not enjoy. Although it wants seven hundred feet of the height of the highest, it yet stands better in several respects than those peaks, which, by their nearness to the monarch himself,

are dwarfed in their apparent proportions. Snowdon is surrounded by the lesser mountains, as by great bulwarks or buttresses to sustain his weight; and instead of standing like most great mountains, as part of a prolonged range or sierra, he is in the centre of a vast heap or agglomeration, and is surrounded by a kind of court, or band of satellites, which stands near him on all sides—north, south, east, and west. Moel Siabod is the eastern outpost.

The ascent is not very difficult from the north or west; but the eastern side is almost perpendicular. Along the edge of the declivity, however, towards the south, is a safe and comparatively easy path, much used by pedestrians for descent. There is a cairn close to the summit. Everywhere the mountain shows the same glossy face, except where, in a kind of amphitheatre, lies the small dark tarn of Llyn-y-foel. On the southern slope is the castle of Dolwyddelan; and this, and the slate quarries, form the two points chiefly interesting in the neighbourhood of Moel Siabod, apart from Snowdon.

Dolwyddelan is situated on a high craggy knoll, one tower only remaining, though two were to be seen in the time of Pennant. There is a portion of the other. "This castle was formerly the residence of Iorwerth Drwyndwn (the Broken Nose), father of Llewelyn the Great, who was born here. The claims of Iorwerth to the throne of Wales were disallowed, in consequence of his deformity. In the time of Henry VII. this district was torn to pieces by the quarrels of rival families and clans." Roscoe says :— "To such lengths did they carry their animosity, that Meredydd ap Ievan is stated to have purchased the castle as a place of defence

within which to retreat from the violence of hi
although the immediate vicinity was beset with
and outlaws. His predecessor, Hoel ap Evan, wa
chief, yet Meredydd did not hesitate to take poss
castle. 'For I had rather,' he exclaimed, 'fight v
thieves than with my own blood and kindred.
my own house at Efionedd, I must either kill my
be killed by them.'"

Higher up the valley is Penamaen, a house b
Meredydd, who also founded the present church,
tombs of his family. Prince Llewelyn ap Yorwer
of whom mention will be found in our notice of B

Within a few miles of Moel Siabod, and ind
his flanks, are several of the famous slate quar
always been objects of interest since their working
upon the present extensive scale. The great Pen
at Nant Francon, a very short distance to the n
many descriptions of them from which we migh
all matters relating to articles of trade and
fluctuations of fashion, and changes in the modes
so frequent and so great, that it would be alm
recognise in the present day the work of ten or a
Fortunately, or unfortunately rather, considera
recently been excited by one of those miserable d
so much to hamper the prosperity of all kinds
country. The contest between capital and lab
quarries will, we trust, be a thing of the past, l
pages are in the hands of our readers. Meanwh

quote from the columns of a London daily newspaper,[*] a pleasantly
written and sufficiently complete account of the slate quarries :—

"How long there has been slate in the mountain of Nant
Francon—better known as the Penrhyn Quarry—is a question for
geologists to decide. But that slate quarried here has been a
marketable article since the reign of Queen Elizabeth is testified by
a document still extant, in which one Sion Tudur writes to Dean
Rowland Tomos, of Bangor, with an order for 3000 slates. A
curious feature about this business transaction is, that it is carried
on in verse, Sion laying himself out in fifty lines, composed in one
of the twenty-four metres which are to this day found barely
sufficient for the need of the Welsh bard. In this cwydd Mr.
Tudur, who dates from Rhyl in the year 1580, informs his
correspondent that he is at the time residing in a house which is
simply thatched, and therefore inconveniently amenable to the
influence of the weather. He begs the Dean to see that the slates
are a fair sample, and they are to be brought down to Aberogwen
(now known as Port Penrhyn), where a ship will convey them to
Rhyl. Finally, in a touching couplet, which brings the interesting
order to a conclusion, Sion prays that the Dean may 'live three
lives,' and that there may be no broken slates in the consignment
from Aberogwen. For more than 200 years after this epistle was
written Nant Francon appears to have been common ground, upon
which anyone quarried at will, or in pursuance of rights, the
foundation of which was, to say the least, hidden in the haze of a
romantic past. Towards the close of the last century, the first
Lord Penrhyn acquired the right of absolute proprietorship in the

* *Daily News*, 5th October, 1874.

mountain, which was then beginning to be well known as containing good slate rock. He speedily put the quarry in regular working trim, and one year cleared as much as £80. To-day, when the quarry is in full work, a million slates are sent down to Port Penrhyn every week, and the wages paid to the quarrymen average from £120,000 to £130,000 a-year."

The writer proceeds to state the rate of wages, and the causes and the effects of the strike, and other things, into which we need not follow him. He also details the rates at which the rock is let to the quarrymen, mentioning that once a-month the stone is apportioned among the men; and goes on to speak of the slate itself, and the form in which it is brought out of the quarry:—

"The quarry is divided into *poncs* or galleries, each bearing a name, generally connected with some event of importance in the Penryhn family. Thus there is the 'Fitzroy,' which was opened about the time Lord Penrhyn married the daughter of the Duke of Grafton; the 'Lord,' which was commenced at the time the peerage was revived in the Pennant family; and the 'Rushout,' a name which has no reference to the sudden desertion of the quarry by the men on the morning of the second strike, but was so called in compliment to the family where the son and heir to the Penrhyn title and estates found his bride. These galleries are on various levels, connected with one another by steps or rope-ladders, up which 'Rover,' a dog that knows more about slate and the general business of quarrying than any other quadruped in England or Wales, gravely climbs in company with the party. Dog and pup, 'Rover' has now dwelt in the quarry for fourteen years, and getting short of breath and being fat withal, has to submit to the indignity

of being helped over the topmost round of the rope-ladder by means
of an umbrella handle inserted in his collar. But in the water
balances no such difficulty arises, and ' Rover ' never misses an
opportunity of making a journey up or down. These ' water
balances' are models of simplicity and mighty power. In course of
time immense banks have been formed at one side of the quarry by
the *débris* of rock and rubble rejected by the quarrymen. These
banks have been levelled, and on them are erected the rows of sheds
where the slates are split and dressed. Over the sides of these
banks is also 'tipped' the countless tons of ' rubbish ' daily made
in the process of getting the slate. But how to get it there ? The
question appears one beside which the historical difficulty of the
apple in the dumpling sinks into insignificance. It is, however,
very satisfactorily answered by an examination of the water
balances. Somewhere near the centre of the bank a shaft is sunk
to the level of the lowest working of the quarry. At the top, level
with the bank and working in a sort of pulley, is a stout chain, to
either end of which is attached a wooden box with a false bottom,
below which is a tank capable of holding five tons of water. The
contrivance is based much on the principle of a pair of scales—
when there is weight in one it goes down to the bottom, and the
other kicks the beam, and *vice versâ*. The weight is supplied by
water brought from the inexhaustible store of a mountain lake, and
turned on at will by a tap from a reservoir. When scale No. 1 is
at the bottom of the shaft, with a four-ton load of slate or rubbish
waiting to come up to the bank, five tons of water is allowed to
rush into scale No. 2, which is at the top, and down it goes, a drop
of 250 feet, bringing up scale No. 1 with a swift, easy motion,

checked by powerful brakes. Then the water-valves are opened, the water rushes out, the scale is loaded, and scale No. 1, coming down with its five tons of water, carries up in its turn scale No. 2. The band is tunnelled from the lowest working level, and a tramway laid down, along which the rubbish and slate blocks are brought, wheeled on to the scale, whirled aloft by the balance, delivered on to another pair of rails, wheeled whither they are wanted, emptied, and so back to the depths again. There are in all sixty miles of tramway, traversing the quarry from every point of the compass, but all converging on the water balances.

"When the slate blocks are delivered in the sheds, the work of splitting and dressing commences. The obliging manner in which a piece of slate splits up on the slightest indication of human desire is at first sight almost miraculous. A man takes a rough block, two or three inches thick, and some two or three feet long by one or two broad. He places at one end of the block a broad chisel, gives it a tap with his hammer, works the chisel about by a motion of his wrist, another tap or two, more motion of the wrist, and lo ! the block is split clean down, as if it had been a conglomeration of cardboard insufficiently amalgamated with paste. This operation is repeated as often as necessary, till the slate is split into pieces of the thickness of those we see on house-roofs. This done, the dresser takes rough pieces of slate in hand, and placing them in a framework, with gauges of the various sizes required, brings down upon them, by the working of a treadle, a huge knife that cuts them as evenly as if they were sandwiches. The various sizes of slates are, throughout the trade, oddly denominated 'Queens,' 'Marchionesses,' 'Duchesses,' 'Countesses,' and 'Ladies.' These

names were given to them in the infancy of the trade, more than a
century ago, by General Warburton; and they now gravely appear
in circulars and prices current. The late Mr. Leicester, a North
Wales county judge, wrote a clever poem on this peculiarity, which
is worth quoting. It runs thus :—

'It has truly been said, as we all must deplore,
That Grenville and Pitt have made peers by the score ;
But now 'tis asserted, unless I have blundered,
There's a man that makes peeresses here by the hundred.
He regards neither Portland, nor Grenville, nor Pitt,
But creates them at once without patent or writ ;
By the stroke of a hammer, without the King's aid,
A lady, or countess, or duchess is made.
Yet high is the station from which they are sent,
And all their great titles are got by descent ;
And where'er they are seen, in a palace or shop,
Their rank they preserve, and are still at the top.
Yet no merit they claim from their birth or connection,
But derive their chief worth from their native complexion.
And all the best judges prefer, it is said,
A countess in blue to a duchess in red.
This countess or lady, though crowds may be present,
Submits to be dressed by the hands of a peasant.
And you'll see when her grace is but once in his clutches,
With how little respect he will handle a duchess !
Close united they seem, and yet all who have tried 'em,
Soon discover how easy it is to divide 'em.
No spirit have they—they're as thin as a rat ;
The countess wants life, and the duchess is flat.
No passion or warmth to the countess is known,
And her grace is as cold and as hard as a stone.
Yet I fear you will find, if you watch them a little,
That the countess is frail, and the duchess is brittle ;

Too high for a trade, yet without any joke,
Tho' they never are bankrupts, they often are broke ;
And tho' not a soul even pilfers or cozens,
They are daily shipped off and transported by dozens !
In France, Jacobinical France, we have seen
How nobles have bled by the fierce guillotine.
But what's the French engine of death to compare
To the engine which Grenfield and Bramah prepare ?
That democrat engine by which we all know
Ten thousand great duchesses fall at one blow ;
And long may his engine its wonders display,
Long level with ease all the rocks in its way,
'Till the vale of Nant Francon of slates is bereft,
Nor a lady, or countess, or duchess is left.'

" When the slates are finished they are loaded into trucks, and sent down by tramway to Port Penrhyn, a distance of six miles. Here there is a splendid pier 800 yards long, round which, in full working service, an average of 30 ships are moored, all busily engaged in loading slates under an organised system, which, like all else in connection with this great undertaking, seems to have solved the great problem of doing the most work in the shortest time, and in the completest manner."

CAERNARVON CASTLE.

THE greatest of the Plantagenets, as Edward the First has been called, though he would probably have disowned the surname, was a man who could not lightly be turned from his purpose. In 1277 he determined on the conquest of Wales. In 1283 he had accomplished his purpose—as far, that is, as it ever was accomplished—by mere force of arms. Centuries had to drag painfully on before the ancient Britons could be subdued to the Anglo-Saxon and Norman invaders of their island; and though Edward, with the foresight of a great ruler, established wherever he could English institutions and laws, he could only overawe the country by vast fortifications, and keep it under his power by an enormous military establishment. Everywhere throughout North and South Wales the Edwardian castles attest his determination, and the persistence with which he carried it through. There are few among them more interesting than Caernarvon, either for historical association, for architectural importance, or for natural beauty of situation.

The admirers of Edward have had much to do to protect his

memory from the charges of severity, and even of cruelty, which
have been brought against him by Welsh and by Scottish historians
and poets. Among these charges, none perhaps is more often made
than that of the massacre of the Welsh bards, and none can be
more easily refuted. Poetry is much to blame for the propagation
of such historical fables. Though the fact may be disproved, the
verse to which it is married is immortal ; and as long as schoolboys
learn to cry—

> " Ruin seize thee, ruthless King,
> Confusion on thy banners wait ;
> Though fann'd by conquest's crimson wing.
> They mock the air in idle state ;"

and so on, the tale will be repeated, even though it be not believed.

> " On dreary Arvon's shore they lie,
> Smeared with gore, and ghastly pale ;
> Far, far aloof the affrighted ravens sail ;
> The famished eagle screams and passes by."

But Gray wanted only to enhance the effect of his ode, and
cared little to clear the reputation of Edward.

It was after the second rebellion of the Welsh that the great
chain of English castles was laid upon Wales. In 1282, David,
brother of Llewelyn whom Edward had subdued four years
previously, attacked, on Palm Sunday, the castle of Hawarden.
He put the garrison to the sword, and carried off the governor,
Roger de Clifford, who, though he was wounded, was loaded with
fetters, and hurried over the mountains to some secret fastness.
David was soon joined by his brother, and overran the Marches,
besieged Flint, and destroyed everywhere the property of the

English with fire and rapine. Edward quickly assembled his army at Rhuddlaw. Here we may quote the narrative of the anonymous author of the *Greatest of the Plantagenets*, though in many particulars he is rather Edward's apologist than his historian :—

"Though insulted and outraged, Edward did not reject the idea of peace. The Archbishop again tendered his services ; and the King permitted him to go to Llewelyn in the hope of bringing him to more reasonable counsels. This attempt proved a fruitless one, but it occupied some weeks. The Welsh prince handed in a list of grievances. They were just such as might have been expected. The country between Chester and Conway, formerly 'debatable ground,' had been ceded to the English, who had established their own laws, and their own courts and judges and officers. The Welsh found themselves in these parts ruled over by men whose language they could not understand. By the Welsh laws, too, great crimes, such as murder or arson, were allowed to be commuted for a fine of five pounds ; while the English courts hanged up the offender. Nor would it be reasonable to assume that the English authorities were at all times patient, and placable, and condescending. It is probable that some causes of complaint really existed ; indeed, considering the position of the two parties, this was nearly inevitable. But the existence of some wrongs of this kind did not make Llewelyn's conduct either wise or reasonable. He had already experienced the King's kindness and generosity ; and he had no right to assume that wrong-doing, clearly shown to exist, would have been maintained and justified. Twice he had been Edward's invited guest in his palace of Westminster ; and he could not doubt of obtaining a patient hearing whenever he chose to carry to the

King's own ear a statement of things requiring amendment. Any course would have been more wise and more defensible than that which was actually adopted, of sudden and treacherous warfare. The Archbishop brought back Llewelyn's answer; but he must have known its insufficiency. Whenever actually engaged in warfare with a subject or vassal, it was Edward's constant rule to listen to nothing but submission. Had Llewelyn applied to him before having recourse to arms, he would readily have done justice; but now, a blow having been actually struck, he demanded, in the first place, submission. That submission he would not purchase by any concession. If Llewelyn would lay down his arms, he should have justice; if not, it must be war, and then 'God defend the right.'

"The summer drew on, and Edward began to move. His path was now quite clear. His vassal, once before rebellious, and then pardoned and generously treated, had now, with greater violence, broken out into open rebellion, and dared his lord to the field. With unhesitating decision, but without any precipitation, the King collected his forces and entered Wales. The plan of the campaign differed in nothing from that of 1277. A naval force was despatched for the reduction of Anglesea. So soon as that island was in the possession of the English, the King's operations were chiefly carried on on the western side of Snowdon. A bridge of boats was constructed for the passage of the Menai Strait; and while this work was in progress, the Welsh, by one of those sudden attacks of which they were always fond, surprised a detachment, commanded by Lucas de Thony, a Gascon knight, and drove it into the Menai, killing and drowning a considerable number of men. Encouraged by this success, and probably dreading to be shut up in Snowdon, as in 1277, Llewelyn left his mountain fastnesses, and passed into Radnor, where he expected to meet a party of friends. He there came into contact with an English force, under the command of Edward Mortimer and John Giffard ; and in an irregular skirmish he was killed by one Adam Frankton, an English soldier, who knew not his person, and was quite unconscious of his rank. But his body was soon recognised by some of the leaders of the party, and the head was cut off and sent to the King. According to the custom of the times, Edward desired it to be forwarded to London, and set up over the gate of the Tower.

"The death of Llewelyn so entirely discouraged the Welsh, that no further opposition was offered ; but the whole principality at once submitted, and became from that day forward an integral part of England. Its annexation was as natural and just a thing as many other annexations which have occurred in our own time. We may go further, and say it was more natural and more just. We have annexed India, under the mild government of Queen Victoria, province after province, of far greater size and population than the principality of Wales, merely because their rulers would not conduct themselves with justice and propriety as friendly and independent states. But Wales had been for centuries feudally subject to England. Edward asked nothing of Llewelyn but that homage and loyalty to which he had an unquestionable right. On Llewelyn's first contumacy, Edward showed the greatest forbearance ; and received his submission, and restored him to his seat, the first moment his submission was tendered. The actual rebellion and open warfare of the Welsh prince against his feudal lord could be visited with nothing less than forfeiture. The chance-medley death of Llewelyn ended the question in the shortest way; but had he met with no such death, the termination of the contest must have been the same. The principality of Wales was forfeited to the superior lord; and Edward could feel no more doubt than we do now, that in uniting the two countries he was consulting the best interests of both. . . . .

"The wretched beginner of this second Welsh controversy, David of Snowdon, succeeded, for several months, in hiding himself in the mountains, and leading the life of an outlaw. His unyielding contumacy completed his ruin. Had he frankly and instantly submitted, and thrown himself on Edward's mercy, all that we know of the King assures us that at least his life would have been saved. But he remained obdurate, until, after a concealment of several months, he was at length given up by some of his own countrymen. Then when there was no longer any merit in submission, and when nothing but an appeal to Edward's mercy could save him, he begged to be allowed to see the King. But Edward was justly and reasonably indignant at his ingratitude, and refused to grant an interview. Still he would not hastily decide upon his fate. No one who has any acquaintance with English history can doubt, that in either of the following ten or twelve reigns, such an offender as this David would have been instantly taken before any convenient tribunal, and would have passed to the scaffold or the gallows in less than twenty-four hours. He was an English subject, he had been raised by Edward to the position of an English earl, and he had requited the kindness by a treacherous rebellion, and by acts unquestionably amounting to high treason."

"He was tried," says the Chronicle of Dunstable, "by the whole baronage of England." It is clear that Edward sincerely desired that others, and not himself, should decide upon the fate of this unhappy man. He appears to have retired to his chancellor's residence at Acton Burnell, about ten miles from Shrewsbury, and to have taken no direct share in the proceedings. The trial took place, and, according to the custom of those days, the criminal was regarded as one who had committed sundry crimes, and who ought therefore to suffer sundry punishment. According to a method which was not uncommon at that period, these crimes and punishments were thus set forth :—" 1. As a traitor to the King, he was to be drawn to the place of execution ; 2. As the murderer of certain knights in the castle of Hawarden, he was to be hanged ; 3. As sacrilegious, in having committed these crimes on Palm Sunday, he was to be disembowelled ; and 4. As having conspired the death of the King in various places, he was to be quartered."

So perished the last sovereign prince of Wales, and such were the circumstances which preceded the erection of Caernarvon, Conway, and other Welsh castles. Fiction has been busy with the subject. The old legends of the massacre of the bards have assumed by degrees the strongest consistency, and other tales equally fanciful and equally near the truth have grown with them. Among these there is one which it is usual to speak of now as entirely exploded. We used always to be told that Edward the Second was born in Caernarvon Castle, and that his father presented him to the Welsh as their native prince. This pretty tale was long repeated, and, for aught we know to the contrary, it is still repeated by the guide to visitors at Caernarvon. Not only are there grounds for doubting

its truth in both particulars, but it is absolutely certain that young
Edward cannot have been born in the Eagle Tower, for a simple
but conclusive reason. Mr. Cliffe (in his *Book of North Wales*)
thus sums up the question :—

"An entirely new light was thrown upon the history of this
great national monument by the Rev. C. H. Hartshorne, at a
meeting of the Cambrian Archæological Association, held at
Caernarvon, in 1848. The whole of the important paper then read
is the result of very long and laborious researches among the
records preserved in London and other places. Mr. Hartshorne
demonstrated 'that the works were commenced at Caernarvon,
10th November, 1284 ; at Conway, 28th October, 1283. That the
walls round the town of Caernarvon were built in 1286, and that
during this year some portion of the castle was covered in with
lead, and extensive works carried on in the fosse. That the castle
was in progress in 1291. That Edward I. entered the town for the
first time, on the 1st of April, 1284, when little had been done at
the castle, the expenses being chiefly confined to the town walls,
and to the fosse round the future castle. *That the Prince of
Wales was born on the 25th of April, 1284, at Caernarvon, but
by no possibility in the Eagle Tower.* That Madoc's insurrection
in 1295 rendered useless all that had previously been erected, and
the works were commenced afresh, beginning at the north-east
angle, from whence, proceeding on the south side, the works were
carried on without interruption. That the records and change of
masonry showed the north side to be of two or three different ages,
the earliest being assignable to some year between 1295 and 1301.
That the Eagle Tower was the work of Edward the Second, shown

by rolls expressly relating to its erection, and by form and character of its mouldings. That the Eagle Tower was roofed in November, 1316; floored in February, 1317; and the great gateway was finished in the 13th of Edward II. (1320); and the Royal effigy over it being then placed there.' Those who are familiar with the previous historical accounts of Caernarvon will see that the foregoing completely destroys them. Among other things it was affirmed, on an authority quoted by Pennant, that the castle was built in one year;—and that Edward II. was *born*, according to received tradition, in the Eagle Tower, is familiar to every one. We confess we regret that the ancient belief should thus be dissipated. The architect of the castle was Henry de Elreton."

Nor was Edward created Prince of Wales at his birth. The real date of the creation is seventeen years later, namely, in 1301. We may share Mr. Cliffe's regrets thus far, that it is a pity a falsehood should have been invented, rather than that, having been examined, its falsity should have been so clearly demonstrated.

The burden cast upon Wales by the conquest may be partly estimated by observing the comparative number and importance of the castles in any district. Along the coast of North Wales, or near it, for example, we have Hawarden, Flint, Rhuddlaw, Dinas Bran, Denbigh, Dinorwig, Dolwyddelan, Criccieth, Dolbadarn, and several more, besides the four attributed usually to Henry de Elreton, Edward's military architect—namely, Caernarvon, Conway, Beaumaris, and Harlech, of which last our initial letter contains a view.

In 1850, Mr. Hartshorne communicated to the *Archæological Journal* a very complete and careful survey of Caernarvon. We venture to extract a few paragraphs, and must refer those of our

readers who desire further information to the paper itself, which
will be found in Vol. VII.

"Immediately after the execution of Prince David at
Shrewsbury, in 1283, Edward I. began to take active measures for
securing the entire possession of the kingdom of Wales; and
amongst the different objects to which his attention was directed,
the erection of fortresses claimed his first consideration. Without
these, indeed, he could retain but a very slight and uncertain
footing in his newly-acquired territory. Within six weeks,
therefore, after the death of the last Welsh prince, he commenced
building the castle of Caernarvon. An entry on the Liberate Roll
of this year authorises the allowance of fifty-four shillings and
eightpence to Roger Sprengehuse, Sheriff of Salop, for the expenses
of forty carpenters sent to Caernarvon; and also of nine pounds
five shillings for 200 footmen, sent from the County of Shropshire
to the same place, for their protection. The Sheriff of Nottingham
was also allowed three pounds two shillings and sixpence for an
equal number of this class of workmen, sent for their assistance
from Nottingham. The Sheriff of Rutland had previously received
his expenses for twenty masons and their foreman, whom he had
sent by the King's command to Conway whilst the monarch was
there, in the 11th year of his reign; thus showing that Conway
Castle preceded Caernarvon, though by but a few months, in the
date of its commencement.

"At the same time that Edward was carrying on these plans
for their coercion, he was not inattentive to the civil rights of the
inhabitants; for having, in the 11th year of his reign, granted a
charter to the people of Caernarvon, in now confirming it, he decreed

that the Constable of his castle, for the time being, should also be Mayor of the borough.

" It is quite impossible, in the absence of any specific evidences, to ascertain what portion of the buildings was first erected ; if, indeed, any part of the existing fabric is really assignable to the period when Edward first began his operations. As we proceed in chronological order, it will be perceived that the work was in a state of progress for several years. The notion, therefore, that the castle was constructed in the short space of twelve months, which has hitherto been the general opinion, is too incredible to engage belief. The extent and magnificence of so vast an edifice could only be the work of a lengthened period. The grandeur of the general design, the stateliness of its lofty polygonal towers, rivalling each other in massiveness and dignity, its long vista of carefully finished corridors, its structures sunk and imbedded in rocky foundations, the ample width and strength of its curtain walls, perforated with every variety of loophole and oilet, and the deep fosse which formerly encircled the northern side, declare at once the utter improbability of such extraordinary works being executed within so limited a period ; perfected, too, at a time when the natives of the country were scarcely vanquished, and when the expenses of the Welsh and Scottish wars had impoverished the Exchequer. . . . .

" From the preceding accounts, it will have been observed that although military works were commenced at Caernarvon very shortly after the death of the last Welsh prince, these operations were in fact extended through a series of years. No particular part of the building is specified at this early period ; and when, therefore, the

King himself visited the place in the twelfth year of his reign, and entered Caernarvon for the first time, on the first day of April, 1284, the accommodation it afforded for himself and Queen Eleanor, then about to give birth to a future Prince of Wales, must have been ill-suited for the reception of royalty. The heir to the English throne was undoubtedly born in the town on the 25th of the same month—whether in the precincts of the castle, or in any particular part of it, it would be hazardous to determine; but, as we shall shortly find sufficient reasons for stating, not in the Eagle Tower, where this event is, by concurrent report, asserted to have happened.

. . . .

" In the twenty-third year of Edward's reign (1295), the affairs of Scotland were so nearly settled, that the English monarch had less cause for anxiety in that quarter. He was about to embark on an expedition on the Continent, being involved in a dispute with Philip IV. of France. His English subjects had readily granted him a fifteenth of their movables; and in his endeavours to enforce a similar tribute from the Welsh, so formidable a revolt broke out simultaneously in three different parts of the principality, that he was obliged to suspend the intended embarkation of his forces, and hasten to suppress the outbreak. The leaders do not seem to have acted together by any preconcerted plan. The rising at Caernarvon happened on a fair-day, when a large concourse of the people were assembled from the surrounding districts, and a great number of Englishmen were collected in the town. Under the command of Madoc, one of Prince David's illegitimate sons, the natives slew all the foreigners; hanging Roger de Pulesdon, the Constable, they plundered and burnt the town, and took the castle. The fastnesses of Snowdon were speedily recaptured, and the unprotected plains of Anglesea fell an easy prey before the arms of the insurgents. The King had now been absent from Wales for eleven years, and during the interval large sums had been expended on the castle ; but the temporary success of the native chieftains placed the monarch in unforeseen difficulties, and compelled him to visit the country immediately. He had first to regain the power that had so suddenly been wrested from his grasp, and to recommence building the great fortress at Caernarvon, which, if not razed entirely to the ground, must have been rendered useless as a garrison. His tenure of Anglesea, too, would require some protection for the future. These transactions will immediately explain the cause of the royal writ on the Clause Rolls of this year, addressed to the Justice of Chester, ordering him to select a hundred masons, and send them immediately to the King's works at Caernarvon, evidently to repair the injuries they had recently sustained ; there to do what Edmund, the King's brother, shall direct ; whilst undoubtedly the castle of Beaumaris owes its origin to the same temporary overthrow of the English power. . . . .

"The tradition of Edward II. having been born in the Eagle Tower has obtained such universal credit, that the assertion has usurped the value of historical truth ; though when we examine the small and highly-inconvenient chamber where this event is said to have happened, it will appear perplexing why so incommodious a room should have been selected, when there were others also in the same tower, and on the same level, more suitable for the Queen's reception. This chamber, both shapeless and low, is a passage to the Vawmer, and is also a thoroughfare to two others of a better kind, as well as contiguous to one of the grand central rooms of the

tower. These circumstances certainly bespeak improbability of
themselves; but the matter is placed out of controversy by the
entries on the present account, strengthened too, as they are, by
some upon a later document, which are preserved in a different
depository of the National Archives. These indisputably prove
that though the Eagle Tower might have been commenced by
Edward I., it was far from being completed when he died; and
there is evidence to show that that portion of the building where
his son is reputed to have been born was actually not built until
the present of the following year, when he was thirty-three years
of age, and had sat ten upon the throne. . . . .

"The castle was commenced at the north-east corner, and
gradually went on to the south-west, the masonry between these
points being apparently the same. Edward I. proceeded with the
works till we reach the lofty curtain-wall to the south-east of the
Eagle Tower, where a string-course indicates the beginning of fresh
operations, whilst the mouldings and masonry henceforward show a
different style. So that the erection of this grand fabric was commenced in the eleventh year of Edward I. (1283), and carried on at
different intervals, till it was advanced to probably its greatest
height of perfection in the fifteenth of Edward II. (1322), thus
extending over a term of thirty-eight years."

The present state of the buildings is better than in most of the
other castles which remain. Caernarvon being Crown property,
has been cared for by the Office of Works, and it has been constantly
kept in a fair state of repair. The castle is only a part of the
general plan of fortification of the whole town, as it occupies the north-
western corner of the walls. There are two quadrangles, marked

only by the different levels, as the dividing wall has disappeared.
No fewer than thirteen polygonal towers break the lines of the walls,
several of them rising to a considerable altitude above the waters of
the Menai and the Sciont. The finest is the Eagle Tower, so called
from the decorations of the battlements being carved with heraldic-
looking figures of spread eagles. It used to be said that these
carvings came from the ruins of the Roman town of Segontium ;
but here again the ruthless antiquarian steps in with the carver's
bills, which were paid by Edward II., for the work. It was also
said that much of the material for the whole building came from
the same ruins ; but here again we have evidence that four hundred
great stones were contracted for in Anglesea, and that a large
number besides were brought over the straits in small vessels.
"The principal entrance into the castle," says Mr. Evans, in the
Beauties of England and Wales, " is peculiarly grand, beneath a
massy tower, on the front of which is a statue of Edward, in a
menacing posture, with a sword half drawn in his hand, apparently
threatening death and destruction to his newly-acquired, yet restive
and reluctant subjects." Another writer says of it, that it "gave
great umbrage to the still smouldering independence of the nation.

'Are ye lead—see ye not where Edward sits ?'

exclaimed a bard in one of his strains, and a thousand hands
quivered on the blades."

Mr. Evans describes the buildings as they appeared fifty years
ago ; and as a good account of what they are now may be found
in the *Guide Book*, we venture to extract the older description, as
now possessing a double interest. It will be observed that Evans
makes all the usual errors in the historical portion of his work :—

"This gate, by the remaining grooves, evidently was defended by four portcullises. The area within is oblong, but of an irregular shape ; and was formerly divided into two parts, forming an outer and inner court. The internal part of this stupendous monument of ancient grandeur is much more dilapidated than would be expected from viewing the outside ; many of the buildings lie in ruinous heaps, and the rooms contained within the towers are mere skeletons. What are called the state apartments appear to have been extremely commodious, lighted by spacious windows, with elegant tracery. These externally exhibit a square front, but internally are all polygonal, some of the sides having been formed out of the thickness of the walls. A gallery, or covered way, appears to have extended completely round the interior of the castle, forming a general communication with the whole of the building : of this about seventy yards are nearly entire. The gate through which the truly duteous and affectionate Eleanor, wife of the conqueror, made her political entry into this proud pile, destined to convert independence into submission—called the Queen's Gate—is considerably above the level of the present ground, and probably was passable only by means of a drawbridge over the moat or fosse. It was defended by two portcullises. The staircase to the Eagle Tower is the only one remaining complete, and from the summit is an extensive view of the surrounding country and the isle of Anglesea. 'Edward the Second,' says Mr. Pennant, 'was born in a little *dark* room in this tower, not twelve feet long, nor eight in breadth : so little did, on those days, a royal consort consult either pomp or conveniency.' On a view of this little *dark* room—which, from its having the accommodation of a fireplace, appears to have

been a dressing-closet—the smallness will strike the beholder at once
with the improbability of its having been prepared for the royal
accouchment. The adjoining central spacious chamber on the same
floor was most probably the one destined by the haughty monarch
for the momentous occasion ; an apartment suitable to the state of
an English queen, and the heir-apparent of a new principality. It
is, however, matter of conjecture, and not worthy of discussion ; for
as Mr. Wyndham justly remarks, 'Surely the birth of such a
degenerate and dastardly tyrant reflects little honour on the castle
of Caernarvon.' "

He makes the following remarks on the dignity of the Prince of
Wales :—"Though Prince Edward was born in 1284, it was not
till he had arrived to his sixteenth year that he received the
reluctant fealty of his deluded subjects. ' In the twenty-ninth year
of that monarch's reign, the Prince of Wales came down to Chester,
and received homage of all the freeholders in Wales. On this
occasion he was invested, as a mark of imperial dignity, with a
chaplet of gold round his head, a golden ring on his finger, and a
silver sceptre in his hand. It is a curious circumstance, that
though the country was transferred by the Welsh, in consequence
of birth, that neither the title nor estate is descendible by birth-
right to the heir-apparent of the British throne. Edward the First
summoned his son to Parliament by the style and title of Prince of
Wales and Earl of Chester ; yet it does not appear that either of
these honours is absolutely hereditary. Edward, subsequent to
that investiture, summoned the same son by the honourable
designation of Earl of Chester and Flint. And when Edward the
Third conferred the principality upon his son, the Black Prince, he

decreed, that in future the eldest son of the kings of England should succeed to the dignity of Duke of Cornwall; and, at the same time, several possessions were annexed to the duchy. Since which time the title of Dux Cornubiæ is legally attached to primogeniture. But long subsequent to that period, the honour of Wales does not appear to have been necessarily connected with *birth*, for the eldest sons of the English monarch were created by letters patent; and though by courtesy the first-born of the royal family is styled Prince or Princess of Wales, yet it does not seem this title is dependent on nativity. However, it is not legally clear, since the time of Henry the Seventh, that any public investiture, by patent or otherwise, has taken place, respecting the honorial distinction; but the eldest son seems to have succeeded, both to the dignity and concomitant property, as a matter of course."

The upper quadrangle contains the Dungeon Tower, in which probably William Prynne was imprisoned, until the number of his sympathisers who visited Caernarvon became so great that he was removed to a more retired place. The town walls were about half-a-mile round, and were formerly defended by twelve turrets and a moat. Evans writes :—

" A walk ranged entirely round the inside of the embattled parapet, and two gates formed the entrance into the town, the east facing the mountains, and the west opening to Menai. A wide and most accommodating terrace, extending from the quay to the north end of the town walls, forms a most charming walk, the fashionable promenade, in fine weather, for all descriptions of people ; who, while they inhale the salutiferous breeze, may be pleasingly amused by the moving varieties of the port."

For the most part, however, the walls have been destroyed or obliterated by private buildings, and can hardly be traced by the visitor. The port, which in Evans's time was of little importance, is now one of the head-quarters of the slate trade, and there is a long pier by the river bank. As many as a hundred thousand tons of slates are brought through Caernarvon in a year.

The remains of Segontium, the Roman station, are "at Llaubelig, within half-a-mile of Caernarvon; the road from Beddgelert piercing the middle. It occupied 'a quadrangular area of about seven acres, on the summit of an eminence gradually sloping on every side, and was defended with strong walls of masonry, of which, on the south side, are extensive portions in a tolerably perfect state.' Several interesting discoveries were made in 1845, in excavating the foundations of a new vicarage house; and others subsequently. A Roman villa and baths have been traced; and a list of coins found includes that most interesting one struck when Judea was subdued, bearing this inscription:—IMP. CAES. VESPASIAN. AVG. P. M. TRPPPCOS. The reverse is not so well preserved, but its legend may be easily traced; the word CAPTA is very legible: Judea is represented sitting under a palm tree, weeping, verifying the prophecy of Isaiah, 'And she, being desolate, shall sit upon the ground.' Near the Seiont was a strong fort, intended to secure a landing-place at high water, two sides of the walls of which are nearly entire. There are traces of other outposts on the opposite side of the Seiont. Ddinas Dinlle, a conspicuous circular artificial mount, of great strength, on the sea-shore, was the chief outpost of Segontium. Coins have been found there."

The compiler of *Murray's Guide* adds:—" The excavations at

98   *Caernarvon Castle.*

this spot brought to light a Roman well or cloaca, where the
vicarage now stands; also portions of a street and hypocaust,
together with numerous coins of the reigns of Domitian, Maximus,
Aurelian, Constantine, and Tetricus. The walls are in tolerable
preservation on two sides, about ten feet in height and six in
thickness. Several outworks kept up the communication,
particularly towards the Seiont, where, 'on the opposite bank,
under Bryn Helen, remains existed to the close of the last century.'
Between them ran the causeway of Helen, or 'Sarn Helen.' . . .
The excavations are now filled up, and the visitors have some
difficulty in tracing the external features of the defences. The
total area of the station was about seven acres. Many of the places
in the vicinity bear the name of Helen, such as Bryn Helen, Sarn
Helen, Ffynnon Helen, Coed Helen, &c. They were so called in
honour of the Princess Helena, daughter of Octavius, the Duke of
Cornwall, and wife of Maximus, first cousin of Constantine, who
was born at Segontium."

The artificial mound mentioned above is evidently a British
work, but it may have been appropriated by the Romans, and
connected with their station at Segontium. It overlooks the sea,
and was strongly fortified with a double line of escarpments. The
sea-line has been considerably injured by the waves, but traces of
watch-towers may be found. The mound was circular, and not less
than four hundred feet in diameter at the base. On the summit is
a large area, surrounded by a vast rampart of earth : within this
space, the remains of buildings, of an oblong form, are discoverable,
constructed with loose stones, and a tumulus composed of the same
materials.

Caernarvon is the county town and a borough, returning one member to Parliament. The population is under 10,000. Its history is closely connected with that of the castle, but presents a few separate features. " In the year 1402, the town was blockaded by a party of insurgents, under the direction of Owen Glyndwr; which was bravely defended for King Henry by Jevan ap Meredydd, to whom, with Meredydd ap Hwlkin Llwyd of Glynllifon, under the command of an English captain, had been committed the custody of the castle. On this occasion so closely was the place invested, that it was found expedient to carry the corpse of Jevan, who died during the siege, by sea, round the peninsular part of the country, for interment at Penmorfa. On the breaking out of the civil wars Caernarvon was seized, in behalf of the Parliament, by Captain Swanley, who, in 1644, took, on the surrender of the town, four hundred prisoners, and a very considerable quantity of arms and ammunition. The royalists, however, appear to have been soon in repossession, for in 1646 it was besieged by the troops under Generals Mytton and Langhorn, to whom it was surrendered upon honourable conditions by the governor, Lord Byron. In 1648, General Mytton was in turn besieged in the town, by a small force under that eminent loyalist, Sir John Owen; but having received intelligence that Colonels Carter and Twisselton were marching with a superior army to relieve the place, he raised the siege, and marched to meet the rebels. Near Llandegai a furious rencontre ensued, in which Sir John was defeated and made prisoner; after which disastrous event, the whole of North Wales submitted to the Parliamentarian authority."

It is highly probable that there was a town of some importance either here or close by from the time of the Romans. Evans, whom we have quoted above, observes on this point :—" But it was in being long previous to that period, and was probably the British town that subsisted under the protection of the Romans, what is now considered the ancient Segontium having been exclusively confined to the use of the Roman military. Giraldus Cambrensis mentions passing through it in the year 1188 ; the author of the life of Gryffydd, the son of Cynan, observes that Hugh, Earl of Chester, who had dethroned the Welsh monarch, and overran nearly the whole of North Wales, to secure his conquests and facilitate future inroads, erected four fortresses—one at Aberllienawg in Anglesea, another in Meirion, a third at Bangor, and a fourth at this place, then denominated *Hên Caer Custenni.* Llewelin the Great also dates a charter, granted to the priory of Penmon, from it in the year 1221. The probability, therefore, is against the idea of the present town having been a creation of the conqueror. To a judicious and able warrior like Edward, however, the place presented a situation admirably adapted for constituting a fortified post, for the purpose of curbing his newly-acquired country. The position was naturally strong, bounded on one side by the Menai Straits, on another by the estuary of the Seiont, on a third by a creek of the Menai, and the remainder has been apparently isolated by art. This fortress, it has been justly observed, from whatever point or from whatever distance it is viewed, assumes a romantic singularity of appearance and an air of grandeur, that, while it excites awe, affords pleasure to the beholder ; and some of its noble walls, going fast to decay, excite a melancholy sigh at the dilapidating powers of hoary-headed time."

MARCUS RAPIDS

BEDDGELERT.

PILLAR OF ELISEG, NEAR VALLE CRUCIS.

F ever a tradition deserved to be treated as a well-proved historical fact, it is the tradition which relates to this beautiful spot. The "grave of Gelert" can hardly have obtained its name from any other source. The tale, as we have it now, may or may not be true; it may have happened a thousand years earlier, or a hundred years later. The tragedy of which it tells is at least so far true, that it unfailingly strikes a tender chord in our hearts; and though the curious in such matters say a similar story is told amongst almost all nations which have any legendary lore, and that various other meanings may be given to the name, we are inclined to agree with the recent writer who says that no one "of the least taste would disturb by doubts so affecting a legend."

We may first give the story in its usual and best form, and next speak of the antiquities and beauties of the place. An accomplished, if not very brilliant poet, the Hon. William Spencer—who, if we mistake not, was one of the bards celebrated in the

famous *Rejected Addresses*—put the fate of Gelert into simple
verses, and we must quote them whole :—

> " The spearmen heard the bugle sound,
>   And cheerly smiled the morn ;
> And many a brach, and many a hound,
>   Attend Llewelyn's horn.
>
> " And still he blew a louder blast,
>   And gave a louder cheer ;
> ' Come, Gelert, why art thou the last
>   Llewelyn's horn to hear ?
>
> " ' Oh, where does faithful Gelert roam ?
>   The flower of all his race ;
> So true, so brave : a lamb at home ;
>   A lion in the chase.'
>
> " 'Twas only at Llewelyn's board
>   The faithful Gelert fed ;
> He watched, he served, he cheered his lord,
>   And centinel'd his bed.
>
> " In sooth, he was a peerless hound,
>   The gift of royal John ;
> But now no Gelert could be found,
>   And all the chase rode on.
>
> " And, now, as over rocks and dells
>   The gallant chidings rise,
> All Snowdon's craggy chaos yells
>   With many mingled cries.
>
> " That day Llewelyn little loved
>   The chase of hart or hare,
> And scant and small the booty proved,
>   For Gelert was not there.

Beddgelert.

" Unpleased, Llewelyn homeward hied :
　　When, near the royal seat,
　His truant Gelert he espied,
　　Bounding his lord to greet.

" But when he gained his castle door,
　　Aghast the chieftain stood :
　The hound was smear'd with gouts of gore,
　　His lips and fangs ran blood !

" Llewelyn gazed with wild surprise,
　　Unused such looks to meet ;
　His favourite checked his joyful guise,
　　And crouched, and licked his feet.

" Onward in haste Llewelyn past,
　　And on went Gelert too :
　And still, where'er his eyes he cast,
　　Fresh blood-gouts shocked his view !

" O'erturned his infant's bed he found,
　　The blood-stained covert rent :
　And all around the walls and ground,
　　With recent blood besprent.

" He called his child ; no voice replied ;
　　He search'd with terror wild ;
　Blood, blood he found on every side,
　　But nowhere found the child !

" ' Hell-hound, by thee my child's devoured !'
　　The frantic father cried :
　And to the hilt the vengeful sword,
　　He plunged in Gelert's side.

" His suppliant, as to earth he fell,
　　No pity could impart ;
　But still his Gelert's dying yell
　　Past heavy o'er his heart.

" Aroused by Gelert's dying yell,
  Some slumberer wakened nigh :
What words the parent's joy can tell,
  To hear his infant cry !

" Concealed between a mingled heap,
  His hurried search had missed ;
All glowing from his rosy sleep,
  His cherub boy he kissed.

" Nor scratch had he, nor harm, nor dread,
  But the same couch beneath
Lay a great wolf, all torn and dead,
  Tremendous still in death!

" Ah ! what was then Llewelyn's pain !
  For now the truth was clear ;
The gallant hound the wolf had slain,
  To save Llewelyn's heir.

" Vain, vain was all Llewelyn's woe :
  ' Best of thy kind, adieu !
The frantic deed which laid thee low,
  This heart shall ever rue !'

" And now a gallant tomb they raise,
  With costly sculpture deckt ;
And marbles storied with his praise
  Poor Gelert's bones protect.

" Here never could the spearman pass,
  Or forester unmoved ;
Here oft the tear-besprinkled grass
  Llewelyn's sorrow proved.

" And here he hung his horn and spear,
  And oft, as evening fell,
In fancy's piercing sounds would hear
  Poor Gelert's dying yell !

" And till great Snowdon's rocks grow old,
And cease the storm to brave,
The consecrated spot shall hold
The name of Gelert's grave."

Such is the story of Gelert as told by Mr. Spencer, and assuredly it is worthy of a poet's best verse. The tomb is still pointed out in a field near the church ; but none of the sculpture mentioned in the ballad remains, if indeed any ever existed upon it. Llewelyn had several children, having been twice married ; and it is not possible now to say which of them was the subject of Gelert's care.

This Llewelyn ap Jorwerth was Prince of Wales, it is said, from 1194 to 1240. The chroniclers detail his deeds at great length ; and we read that in the latter year "the most valiant and noble prince, which brought all Wales to his subjection, and had so often put his enemies to flight and defended his country, enlarging the mears thereof further than they had been many years before, passed out of this transitory life, and was honourably buried at the Abbey of Conway, after he had governed Wales well and worthily fifty and six years." His second wife was Joan, a daughter of King John of England, by whom he was father of David, who succeeded him. This prince died childless, and the descendants of his father's elder son, Griffith, were the princes whose sad end, under Edward the First, is detailed in our account of Caernarvon.

Some authorities say that Llewelyn founded the church at Beddgelert in memory of the rash deed narrated in Mr. Spencer's poem ; but it is certainly older than his time, though he probably was a great benefactor to the monastery of the " Blessed Mary of Snowdon" at this place, which was a place of resort for pilgrims, especially those passing and repassing to and from Ireland. The church is very curious, being of the age of Edward the First; and though small, possesses some points of interest, the chancel being lighted with three tall lancet windows, and the arches, which formerly communicated with a north aisle, remaining built up into the wall. Portions of the cloisters may also be seen; but the monastery was destroyed, or at least severely injured, by fire in 1289. According to Mr. Evans, "Edward the First, by his sole munificence, repaired the damages; and Bishop Anian, as an inducement for benefactors to come forward and enable the prior to use his accustomed hospitality, remitted by an indulgence forty days of any penance they might previously have been enjoined for past transgressions. It was given by Henry the Eighth, in 1535, to the Abbey of Chertsey, in Surrey; and the annual revenues at the Dissolution amounted, by Dugdale's valuation, to £72 8s. 8d.; by Speed's, to £69 3s. 8d. No part of the building now remains, but it is probable the present church has at times been repaired out of the ruins.

"The village consists of a few straggling cottages; and one, little distinguished from the rest, was, a few years past, the only place where the traveller could obtain refreshment. He will now find a comfortable inn, with excellent accommodation, whether he proceeds on horseback or in a carriage; and a more pleasing or convenient station he cannot take for making excursions to some of the most interesting scenes in this and the adjacent county."

Mr. Cliffe gives the following description of the scenery in the neighbourhood of Beddgelert:—" We know not how to account for it, but Beddgelert never, to us, fully realised its early promise, although it has always been one of the favourite resorts of tourists ; perhaps it is too much enclosed. In colour it has few equals. The road below the Goat Hotel leads along the vale through which the united rivers flow into the ravine called Pont Aberglaslyn—the gate into Merionethshire. Here a vast rent has been made in the body of the mountain ; the precipitous sides of the chasm rise in sombre majesty to the height of 700 feet, and at the bottom the river works for itself a narrow channel among innumerable masses of rock, torn by the convulsions of nature or the force of the elements from the crags above. The schistose rocks of which the mountain is composed are in some places perfectly black ; in others grey ; in others of an ochry tint, betraying the richness of their internal veins ; in some of them grassy mosses and lichens flourish ; there is much heath ; and frequent tracks of torrents, with continual heaps of *débris*, intersect the sides, or project into the stream. The east side, on which the traveller's eye necessarily dwells, is the most abrupt and tremendous of the two ; the other, more prolific in its mineral contents, has a vein of copper which has been successfully worked, and bears several plantations on its more gentle declivities ; the road, too, has been constructed along it, and winds through the pass for about half-a-mile. In so short a space the river experiences a considerable descent, rushing along with vast rapidity and noise ; and where the surface of the water is not broken into waves or covered with foam, a great variety of tints, green and brown of every shade, are reflected back by the rocks through the transparent fluid. Whether visited in the sunshine of the morning, or by the pale rays of the moon ; in the heat and dryness of summer, when

the river is diminished in strength; or amidst the snows and rains
of winter, at which season it becomes a furious torrent, disdaining
its former bounds, and filling to a great depth the bottom of the
chasm, the Pass of Pont Aberglaslyn will always present a picture
of the highest sublimity. The lofty steepness of the rocks on either
side, their sterility and dark, damp colour, the narrowness of the
chasm, and the roaring fury of the river, cannot fail at all times
powerfully to impress the mind. The traveller will never hurry
through this wonderful spot; he will always pause at that point
where the vales at both ends of the pass are shut out from his
view; and if the moon be shining over the mountain, lighting up
the recesses of the rocks, and twinkling in the stream below, his
lingering steps will scarcely lead him from so fine a scene.

"The Glaslyn emerges from the ravine beneath a bridge, pours
its waters between rocky walls and wooded banks for a short
distance, and at length flows in a silent expanded stream, through
the Vale of Tremadoc, to the sea."

Mr. Evans has also given some charming descriptions, one of
which relates to the country to the north-east of Beddgelert, and
the Pass of Nant Gwynant in particular. "It affords," he says,
"such multifarious scenery, composed of luxuriant meads, watered
by expansive lakes, whence issue numerous streams, that meander
towards the sea; and circumvented by august boundaries, finely
clothed with wood far up their sides, above which they lift their
bare and rugged summits to the skies in all the diversity of
colouring; so that the beauty and order, so admirably described by
the elegant Mason, are here actually exhibited to the enraptured
view.

" ' Vivid green,
Warm brown, and black opake, the foreground bears
Conspicuous. Sober olive coldly marks
The second distance. Thence the third declines
In softer blue, or lessening still, is lost in
Faintest purple.'

"About a short mile up this valley, on the left, rises a lofty rock, forming part of the mountain barrier, on which it is said Vortigern had his residence previous to his final retreat from the persecutions of his subjects to Nant Gwrtheyrn, in the vicinity of Nefyn. This he bestowed upon his favourite soothsayer, Ambrosius; and the spot still retains the appellation of *Dinas Emrys*, or the Fort of Ambrosius, called in Welsh *Merddin Emrys*. On the top of this precipitous rock is a considerable area, the accessible part of which. is defended by two large ramparts: within this are the remains of a stone-building, about ten yards in length ; and the walls, though built without mortar, appear very thick and strong. Near this, a place, allusive to the magical story of Vortigern and his court, is called *Cell-y-dewiniaid*, or the cell of the Diviners.

" Here, ' Prophetic Merlin sate, when to the British king
The changes long to come, auspiciously, he told.
And from the top of Brith, so high and wondrous steep
Where Dinas Emris stood, showed where the serpent fought,
The *white* that tore the *red*, from whence the prophet wrought
The Briton's sad decay, then shortly to ensure.' *

"This Merddin is represented in legendary story as the son of a vestal virgin, begotten by an *incubus;* consequently endued with

* Drayton's *Poiyolbion.*

miraculous and predictive powers; and numerous prophecies are attributed to him, the copying or recital of which was prohibited by the Council of Trent. But the traveller will pleasurably turn away from the recollection of such absurdities, to view the beautiful Llyn-y-Dinas, filling the vale with its expansive waters; favoured for a large and well-flavoured trout; and affording the effects of contrast and vividity to the surrounding scenery. Two miles beyond this rise, with unwieldy bulk, Y Aran, under which is a romantic hollow, denominated Cwm Llan, extending on the left towards Snowdon, whose summit is here finely visible between the intervening mountains. Numerous trees, issuing out of the rocky clefts at the feet and sides, tend greatly to relieve the eye from the fatiguing, dull uniformity of the mountain. At the same time a neat modern mansion, embosomed in woods, with a small lawn in front, forms a fine close to the upper end of the lake. The mountains here converge, but soon recede; and another lake, Llyn Gwynant, presents itself to view. This is about three-quarters of a mile in length, and nearly fills the valley, leaving little more than space for the continuation of the road."

A writer in the *Guardian* newspaper, of September 9, 1874, considers Beddgelert one of the best places from which to ascend Snowdon. He says:—"Snowdon was, of course, in our programme. In shape, as well as in height, Snowdon is fairly monarch of the Welsh mountains: there are no finer hollows than those which his six arms embrace; no uglier or more saw-like ridges than those which enclose his hollows; no more charming little lakes than those basined at different heights in his sides. Of all the several ways up Snowdon, that from Llanberis is the tamest. By

far the most imposing approach is that from Capel Curig, by way
of Gorphwysfa; but that from Beddgelert is also fine; and, after
seeing the mountains thoroughly, I should say that an ascent from
Beddgelert, and a descent to Gorphwysfa, will show its features
best. Ascent or descent by the Crib Goch ridge, or by Bwlch-y-
Saethan, is dangerous: on the former route, in particular, a man's
life depends upon his not slipping or stumbling.

"Ascending Snowdon from Beddgelert, the first aim is to get
fairly upon the mass of the mountain at Llechog, a recurved ridge,
which, like all the six arms (some places excepted), has one
precipitous and one rounded side. Llechog is precipitous towards
the north, but easily accessible on the other side. Arriving upon
Llechog, you look down into one of Snowdon's hollows, Cwm-y-
Clogwyn, another of the characteristic spoon-shaped valleys, though
not the finest in Wales. You hem the precipitous edge of Llechog
for awhile, looking over into impossible precipices, or down at
barely traversable loose slopes; you serpentine the more solid piece
of the slope; presently you come up upon the narrow bridge which
leads from Llechog to the summit, called Bwlch-y-Main. This is
another situation of grandeur beyond imagination without seeing.
Here are deep spoon hollows on both sides; on one hand Cwm-y-
Clogwyn, on the other the longer and broader deep of Cwm-y-Llan.
Sometimes the path, which winds about among sharp, jagged rocks
set upright, and forming an edge not many feet wide, passes the
brink of Cwm-y-Clogwyn; then you go through a notch in the
jagged edge, and see down into Cwm-y-Llan. As you clamber
along this ridge (which looks a most frightful place, but is really
perfectly safe, and is sometimes done with ponies), you see the top

of Snowdon, with the hut, rising among the jags above you ; the last part of the climb is truly magnificent.

" But the full grandeur of Snowdon cannot be better seen than from the steep and difficult (but not in the least dangerous) path to Gorphwysfa. The sun was out as we descended; but frequent clouds came to shade the path, and we went merrily down towards Capel Curig, with a midland woolspinner, who thought he had done great things in mountaineering to walk up the easy ride from Llanberis, but was quite willing to learn better, and seemed fairly awe-struck at the majesty of Snowdon on the way down to Gorphwysfa, sharing also our delight with that pretty green lake which lies highest and closest to the mountain's side."

Mr. Cliffe (*Book of North Wales*, p. 179) thus describes the same ascent :—" One evening in June we reached Beddgelert with two friends. . . . The next morning . . the clouds were down on Snowdon ; but Moel Hebog, which is a sort of barometer for its huge neighbour, gave promising signs. ' It *may* clear off, sir, indeed, when we get up.' Thus cheered, we started, walking for about two and a-half miles on the Caernarvon road before we turned off, not far from ' Pitt's Head,' a rock on the roadside, with a profile resembling that immortal statesman. Leaving a farm-house, *Fridd-Uchaf*, we kept near a torrent on our right, the summit of Snowdon bearing, we were told, north-east. The peak of Aran, with its long serrated curtain, rose on the east. After steady collar-work for about two miles, we began to shake off Cwm Craigog, and halted at a delicious spring, where our guide's canteen and our flasks of brandy were serviceable, the old guide beguiling the time with a store of anecdotes—one of which, of a wild Irishman who insisted on ascending in winter, and did ascend, when Snowdon was rather thickly covered with snow, struck our fancy much. Soon after we came in sight of a profound hollow, penetrating the very heart of the mountain, *Cwm-y-Clogwyn,* or "The Precipice," in which four small pools, called *Ffynnon Lâs, Llyn Gôch, Llyn Ffynnongwas,* and *Llyn-y-Nadroedd* (signifying severally the Blue, the Red, the Servants', and the Adders' Pools), sullenly repose. The depth, the gloom, the severity of this great hill solitude impressed us powerfully. The clouds continued most tantalising. Now there was a sudden lift, then vast masses of vapour swooped down upon us, filling Cwm-y-Clogwyn in an instant; again the grey mass rose, gracefully playing with the rocky outworks of the dread hidden mountain citadel. Ponies are left near the spot on which we stood. We had Warner's description of the terrors of the *Clawdd Gôch* fresh in our mind as we entered on the passage of that red ridge. The scene was indeed awe-inspiring. The clouds came down again ; the soughing of the wind was full of inexpressible melancholy ; the dim light exaggerated the fearfulness of the depth—you *felt* that a false step would be fatal. Yet in broad sunlight the prospect is sublime. Bingley thought that in some parts of this narrow stony *bwlch,* if a person held a large stone in each hand, and let them both fall at once, each would roll above a quarter of a mile, and thus when they stopped be more than half-a-mile asunder ; and he does not exaggerate. Below us, on the east and north-east, but hidden by the mist, were Llyn Llydaw and Glaslyn—the former filling the bottom of a dark 'cwm' one and a-half miles long. After treading carefully over the slippery rocks for several hundred yards, at last we made out the Ordnance mark through the gloom, and approached the Wyddfa. Not a soul was there. We stood alone on the highest spot in the British isles south of the Forth. The damp of the clouds, the chilly mysterious wind, the darkness ceased not. We could only see a few yards on either side; and even the faith of our old guide in the day was sometimes much shaken. Presently we heard him shouting in Welsh to some one, and found that one of the Llanberis guides was in advance of a party. Suddenly the dull vapours began to break at several points, and we obtained magical glimpses of distant scenes, which had a dream-like effect. Sunny mountain lakes flitted like diamonds across our vision, in the swift wavy line of clouds; then a wandering glory lit up a grand peak, or disclosed a gentle hill solitude; now all Anglesea, like a variegated carpet, was visible; the proud towers of Caernarvon, the green ocean, swelling hills, silver mountain threads, were illuminated or hidden by turns; darkness followed. About half-an-hour was thus spent in a state of excitement; and in the meanwhile other parties had arrived, and more than a dozen shivering mortals clustered round the narrow top. There were no huts—which have spoiled the romance of this height—then; no shelter but the modern cairn. Suddenly, swift as thought, the whole mass of cloud sailed off Snowdon! and before us and around us, bathed in sunshine, were landscapes which, once seen, can never be quite blotted out—

"'Meditation here may think down hours to moments.'"

Marcus Ward & Co., Printers, Royal Ulster Works, Belfast.

www.ingramcontent.com/pod-product-compliance
Lightning Source LLC
Chambersburg PA
CBHW030543270326
41927CB00008B/1490